DIXIE BROWNING
Wren of Paradise

Silhouette *Romance*

Published by Silhouette Books New York

Distributed in Canada by PaperJacks Ltd., a Licensee of the trademarks of Simon & Schuster, a division of Gulf+Western Corporation.

Other Silhouette Romances by Dixie Browning

Chance Tomorrow
Tumbled Wall
Unreasonable Summer

SILHOUETTE BOOKS, a Simon & Schuster Division of
GULF & WESTERN CORPORATION
1230 Avenue of the Americas, New York, N.Y. 10020
In Canada distributed by PaperJacks Ltd.,
330 Steelcase Road, Markham, Ontario.

ISBN: 0-671-57073-0

First Silhouette printing April, 1981

10 9 8 7 6 5 4 3 2 1

America's Publisher of Contemporary Romance

Printed in Canada

"Who Are You? What's Going on Here?"

Hannah struggled to her feet, turned and immediately flinched at a blast from arctic blue eyes. The man looked past her to the broken artifact on the floor, and in two swift strides was pinning her against the table with his intimidating size.

"It didn't occur to me to lock this door, even when Jill told me a relative of hers had dropped in for an unexpected visit. For the short time you remain you will confine yourself to the public areas of the *casa* and avoid my private quarters!"

Hannah was speechless. She wasn't responsible for the destruction of the artifact. But all the same, how dare he imply that she was an unwelcome visitor!

"You don't have to worry, *señor!* I'll confine myself right out of your precious Casa Azul."

DIXIE BROWNING
grew up on Hatteras Island off the coast of North Carolina. She is an accomplished and well-known artist of watercolors, as well as a prolific writer.

Dear Reader:

Silhouette Romances is an exciting new publishing venture. We will be presenting the very finest writers of contemporary romantic fiction as well as outstanding new talent in this field. It is our hope that our stories, our heroes and our heroines will give you, the reader, all you want from romantic fiction.

Also, you play an important part in our future plans for Silhouette Romances. We welcome any suggestions or comments on our books and I invite you to write to us at the address below.

So, enjoy this book and all the wonderful romances from Silhouette. They're for you!

Editor-in-Chief,
Silhouette Books,
330 Steelcase Road East,
Markham, Ontario L3R 2M1

Chapter One

It had been raining dismally when she changed in Miami, so there was no in-between stage, nothing to prepare her for the stunning assault of brilliance when she stepped off the Mexican airliner in Cozumel.

Can this really be me—plain old Hannah Blanchard from the foothills of North Carolina? Hannah looked about her with wide, amazed eyes, taking in the exotic shrubs blooming with what seemed to her an indecent extravagance under a pink and turquoise sky.

The other passengers had disappeared into the small airport and Hannah hurried after them, suddenly overcome with feelings of vulnerability. For the first time in her life she was over a thousand miles from all that was familiar, and when the baggage cart rolled past her, with its driver and his assistant chattering away in a rapid Spanish that bore no resemblance to the language she had learned ages ago in high school, she felt totally alien and alone.

Against the comparative dimness inside the terminal she searched for Jill's bright head as she followed the others through the formalities. As usual, Jill was late. Bringing her momentary panic under control, Hannah sat down on one of the plastic chairs and peered shyly at the mixture of laconic Mexicans and the tourists who fell into two categories— eager and excited or determinedly blasé.

It was optimistic and unrealistic to expect Jill to be on time, but then the letter that had started the whole unlikely thing had been out of character and Hannah was ever the optimist.

As she waited for her stepsister to meet her, Hannah thought back to the time she had first waited for her. Jill had been Jill Grainger then, instead of Jill Tolland. Hannah's mother had just announced her plans to marry Ed Grainger, Jill's father, and Jill had been coerced into giving up her plans for the afternoon to come out to the farm and meet her future family. Hannah had been ten then and Jill a very sophisticated sixteen, and at the first glimpse of those exquisite features, the long, blond hair, and pale blue eyes, Hannah had had an intuitive knowledge of the relationship that was to grow between the two of them.

She had not been far wrong. Jill, socially successful and infinitely poised, had had little time for a small, chubby girl from a tobacco farm. Hannah at ten was not all that different from Hannah at seventeen, when the two of them had shared an apartment in town—still lacking in inches, a little too rounded ever to be considered fashionable. Cute, Bill had called her, like a little brown wren—his nut-brown maid. She had no illusions about her looks, the straight hair and eyes both the color of dried leaves and a pale, fine-textured skin that tanned at the first hint of spring. She was infinitely overlookable, and that was why it had thrilled her so when Bill Tolland, the photography instructor at the community college, had started taking her out.

Jill had been twenty-three then, working as a cosmetics demonstrator for a well-known line, and the two girls got along well enough in the small apartment they had rented after Ed Grainger moved out west. Hannah's mother had died the year before and there was nothing to hold them together except mutual convenience.

Worriedly, Hannah consulted her watch. She had been here for almost forty-five minutes now and she wondered if she should try to call—what was his name? Lucas? No—Lucian Trent. She decided to give it another fifteen minutes. This was the land of *mañana*,

after all. Jill had not mentioned how long she
had been here in Mexico, but evidently it was
long enough to pick up that particular trait.

Jill. It had been two and a half years since
Hannah had seen her stepsister. After Bill's
defection, they had gone their separate ways,
keeping in touch with the occasional letter or
card.

Not that it was a defection, really. Bill and
Hannah had not been engaged, or anywhere
near it. After all, at seventeen—and a very
young seventeen, at that—she had only been
trying out her wings. Bill was ten years older,
a kind, amusing man, attractive in a puckish
sort of way—the type who could make a shy,
chubby little wren feel like a bird of paradise.

He had taken one look at Jill and gone down
without a whimper. Jill, of course, had not
actually *done* anything—all she had to do was
be there, looking as if she had stepped off the
cover of a glossy magazine.

That had been the start, the first domino.
Bill, as a professional photographer, had seen
her potential, and within six months he had
her portfolio—compiled by himself, of
course—circulating in New York and was
managing her budding career as a model. The
marriage was almost incidental. Hannah had
always wondered why Jill had married him,
but as far as Bill was concerned, there was
never any doubt—he was smitten for good.

Well, here it was, four-twenty in the afternoon on Isla de Cozumel, Territory Quintana
Roo, Mexico, and Hannah Blanchard was

beginning to feel distinctly uneasy. For the
first time it occurred to her that something
might have happened to prevent her from
being met. No, surely someone would have
called if that were the case. Could it be that
Jill had changed as much as Hannah herself
had in two and a half years? Of course, the
change in Hannah had been recent and strictly a by-product of a long, debilitating siege of
flu, followed by pneumonia. She had been
trying to work full time and go to school at
night and it had been too much. In the end,
she had lost her job, her apartment, and
seventeen pounds, leaving her almost a
stranger to herself.

She had remained friends with Bill Tolland
and his mother, Rosa, even after Jill had
divorced Bill and gone on with her career as a
model, and when Hannah was about to go
under without a trace it had been Bill and
Rosa who had stepped in to do a rescue and
repair job. They insisted she move into their
guest room where Rosa could look after her
and fatten her up again, and although the
pounds had not returned, her strength had
and she had been actively engaged in looking
for work again when Jill's letter had come,
forwarded from the apartment, to invite her to
Cozumel.

Rosa had been against it; Bill, oddly
enough, was very much in favor of it, and
Hannah had been easy to persuade. He had
reasoned that even now she was not completely her old self and that a chance to escape a

dreary, cold January was not to be dismissed lightly. In the end, he had prevailed and Hannah had written Jill to tell her when she would arrive.

It had taken every bit of her savings—not that there was much left after her illness—plus a small loan from Bill to get her by bus to Miami and by air to Cozumel, and with the small hoard of traveler's checks she hoped to buy enough summery things to replace the ones that no longer fit. All she had been able to resurrect had been three shifts and a couple of smock tops to go with the new jeans she had bought. It wasn't easy to buy summer clothes in the middle of winter in Winston-Salem.

"Hannah?" The voice was familiar, even though the tones were strained, almost shocked.

"Jill! I thought you'd forgotten me!" Hannah exclaimed, jumping up to throw her arms around the exquisite creature who had appeared at her side. Jill looked even lovelier than she remembered her, her hair still the same impossible shade of moonlight blond, cropped now into a petal cut that was infinitely becoming.

"Good Lord, what have you done to yourself? You look gaunt!"

"Thanks," Hannah replied wryly, gathering up her small case and the sweater she had worn on the first leg of her trip. Bill had taken her coat back with him when he drove her to the bus station, for she absolutely refused to carry any such reminder of the sleety weather she was leaving behind.

"Come on out to the car—we can talk there. Is this all? You do travel light, don't you?"

The car was a pale blue jeep with a candy-striped canopy and Jill apologized. "It goes with the *casa* and Lucian refuses to bring a decent car over to the island. Says they don't last in the salt air. But this thing is ridiculous! It looks like an overgrown golf cart!"

"I love it! It's perfect! Oh, Jill, I can't believe I'm actually here! I've been brushing up on my Spanish all the way and I tried it out on one of the stewardesses. I asked her a question I had memorized from the book, but I couldn't understand a word she said. The book didn't give the answers, only the questions. I have a lot to learn."

"So have I," Jill remarked, and something in her voice caused Hannah to look at her more closely. Jill had seldom bothered to hide her displeasure and for some reason she was definitely not pleased at the moment.

"What is it—has something happened?" Hannah asked. "Isn't it convenient for me to visit right now?"

Jill maneuvered the frivolous-looking vehicle onto a wide clearing overlooking an impossibly blue sea and switched off the engine. "Oh, it's convenient, all right," she said candidly. "If there is one thing I'm not cut out for, it's baby-sitting, and you, Hannah dear, were to be the answer to my prayers. The only thing is, I thought you were still a duckling and at

Casa Azul there's only room for one swan—
me!"

Hannah blinked, not entirely because of the
abundant sunshine. "But you don't mean—
you can't mean—"

"I mean, dear headstrong, headlong
Hannah"—she drawled out the taunt that had
followed Hannah through the years—"that in
spite of that awful hairstyle, in spite of the
nine-ninety-eight special you're wearing, and
in spite of that touchingly pale complexion,
you've turned into a good-looking female, so I
think I'd better lay out a few ground rules
before we go any further, just in case you get
any ideas." She fitted a cigarette into a Lucite
holder and flicked a jeweled lighter. "Lucian
Trent is mine. Strictly a no-no where you're
concerned, understand? Oh, not that he'd
give you a second look—you're not *that* great-
looking. It was just the change that threw me
for a minute—all those bones instead of the
comfy little dumpling. How'd you do it, jog all
day and live on lettuce and bean sprouts?"

"Would you believe flu, followed by pneumonia?" Hannah laughed shakily. Suddenly
the sun didn't seem to be shining as brightly.

"Oh, sorry, hon. No wonder you snapped up
my offer. I wasn't even sure when I wrote that
you'd be free. What happened to your job?"

"It was a casualty. It wasn't all that great,
really, but it paid well enough so I could
afford the night school. Now that's all fouled
up, too. Missed too much of the term."

"Well, you'll have a job out here, never fear!

The pay is room and board plus my eternal gratitude and the job is keeping two little hellions named Kip and Alice. They're Lucian's. He was married to Larice Graylon, remember? She starred in his first big hit, *All's Fair*."

"Jill, you'll think I'm stupid, but I can't even think who Lucian Trent is. I don't go to a lot of movies or watch much television. Homework, you know."

"Oh, I'd forgotten what a provincial little duckling you were. Lucian Trent, for your information, is one of London's leading playwrights, as well as the most gorgeous creature on two continents. His mother was Mexican, left him acres and acres of something agricultural and dull, and his father was English. Lucian was raised in Mexico but he went to school in England and started writing there. Anyhow, he leased this place here on the island when he got custody of the children after Larice died and hired a governess to help the old couple with them. The governess came down with something dreary that required surgery and a long recuperation, and out of the goodness of my heart I offered to come along and help Lucian look after his brood." She shuddered, an exquisite motion of shapely shoulders. "Only it takes a bit more than I'd figured on. I thought the old couple who came with the house would do most of it, but they're ancient and so—here you are— *voilá!* I remembered my sweet, obliging little stepsis, who probably hadn't had a decent vacation in years, and it all worked out just perfectly. You need the sunshine, I need your help. Fair trade, right? Only one thing—don't get any ideas about Lucian being one of the fringe benefits. I intend to be the next Mrs. Trent."

Hannah felt confused, flattened, and almost sorry she had come, although what else she had expected, she couldn't say. After all, Jill certainly hadn't misled her about the reason for her generosity. Well, not much, anyway. She had to say something. The older girl was waiting expectantly for a reaction. "What happened to the first one?" she asked, not really caring.

"Oh, they were divorced and she went out to Hollywood, then she was in that crash—you remember the headlines? They were married when they were both just kids. Larice used Lucian for a stepping stone and then dropped him for Oliver Hayes. They were having an affair, anyway, everybody said, and—"

Hannah interrupted. "It doesn't matter. I don't keep up with that set and the names don't mean a thing to me." But she couldn't help but think of the similarity of the two cases: Larice and Lucian, Jill and Bill.

As if reading her thoughts, Jill asked about her ex-husband. "Do you ever see Bill these days? I understand he's back in the area, working out of High Point for the furniture market. Your new looks didn't do you much good there, did they?"

"As a matter of fact, when I got sick and fell

behind on my rent, Rosa and Bill invited me to stay with them until I was on my feet again. Bill's doing really well. At least, he's a lot happier than he was in New York."

"Miaow," Jill mocked, but she was staring out over the Caribbean as if her thoughts were a thousand miles away. "Everyone thought I married him just so I could have cocktail napkins with Jill and Bill on them, did you know that? Ha! Poor Bill's idea of a cocktail was sweet wine with ginger ale!"

"Yes, well, he may not be the world's most sophisticated man, but he's been absolutely marvelous to me. I don't know what I'd have done without him and Rosa."

"But then you always were in love with him, weren't you?"

"No. I love him, but as a brother. It was never more than that, even before—"

"Before I snaffled him from under your turned-up little nose? Well, if you say so. All the same, you're living with him now. Oh, all right, with him and his mama, but just remember—you can have Bill if you want him, but hands off my Lucian." With that she started the engine and backed out onto the paved road that ran along the edge of the beguiling sea.

Casa Azul was almost too perfect. Before she recalled that Lucian Trent was only leasing it, Hannah's immediate reaction was that it was exactly what a playwright, someone lionized on both sides of the Atlantic, might choose. But then her innate sense of fair play took over and she admitted that the whole island was theatrical-looking to someone who had never strayed more than two states from home before.

As she was reaching to pull her case out of the jeep, twin dervishes erupted from an arched opening in the pale blue stucco to disappear in the lush growth that surrounded the sprawling building.

"You're being vetted," Jill remarked dryly, waiting for Hannah to gather up all her belongings.

"Vetted?"

"Looked over. Ignore them—they'll be upstairs before we are."

There seemed to be no one about and Hannah followed Jill hesitantly across the darkly gleaming floors. The whole salon seemed cool, dark, and spacious, and even to Hannah's unsophisticated eyes most of the furnishings looked like valuable antiques. There was a faintly Moorish look to the place, with its archways and columns, and when she almost tripped on one of the opulent rugs, Jill chided her.

"Stop rubbernecking, goose, or I'll tell everyone I got you from lost and found! Carlotta's out in the kitchen and Lucian won't be in until later on tonight. You'll have plenty of time to settle in and get acquainted with the kids. I've put you in their section, by the way. We're situated around the courtyard here, with a bedroom wing on each side, and you go into the governess's room. Lucian and I, of course, are across the way. Quite a pad, isn't it?"

"It's marvelous, Jill, but you and—I mean, did you mean that you and Mr. Trent are—"

"And what if we are, sweetie? It's no concern of yours. Here." She opened a richly carved door and gestured for Hannah to precede her. "You might want to clean up and change. Carlotta feeds the kids in the kitchen, thank heaven, so they'll be out of our hair. Meet you in the courtyard in about an hour and a half."

Despite certain misgivings, Hannah prowled the room eagerly. There were two balconies—one that looked out over a shadowy courtyard and another, on the outer side, that overlooked the woods and the sea beyond. The room was lovely, its floors a parquet of contrasting woods, the furniture massive and carved. Draperies and spread were of a tapestrylike material of brick, beige, and black and against one stark, white wall, a stylized landscape glowed in the light of the setting sun.

She found the bath that she was to share with the children and soaked most of the tiredness from her bones as she made an attempt to organize her wildly varied impressions. Maybe she had been overhasty in coming here when she hadn't seen Jill in so long. It wouldn't be the first time she had leaped first and looked later, but this was a pretty big leap.

Slipping on her inexpensive cotton duster,

she straightened up the bathroom and reen-
tered her bedroom, stiffening at the sound of
quickly muffled laughter. With only the
slightest hesitation, she proceeded to let her
hair down and tug a brush through it, studying the armoire behind her in the mirror. Sure
enough, the door opened a crack, then more,
and two solemn faces peered out at her.

Hannah's hair hung well below her waist
and she was not really pretending when she
muttered impatiently, "I only wish I had
someone to reach the back for me."

The faces emerged further; Hannah flung
the tan mop over her shoulder and com-
menced dragging the brush through again. "I
just can't get the very back," she fussed,
ostensibly to herself.

"I could reach it for you," piped a clear
young voice in an accent that sounded oddly
adult to ears more used to a Southern drawl.

"Me too! I could do it, too, Alice!"

By the time Hannah was ready to go downstairs, she had listened to countless disclo-
sures from two eager young minds, learned
that a piñata was even better than stockings
on a mantel and that Santa Claus came
ashore on Cozumel on waterskis. The two
children, five-year-old Kip—Christopher Peter
Trent—and six-and-a-half-year-old Alice Lucy
Trent, assured her that she *could* drink the
water here at Casa Azul—"That means blue
house," Kip informed her importantly—and
that tomorrow they would show her their very
favorite places.

So much for the vaunted British reserve, Hannah thought with a grin. Maybe it was the combination of Mexican sun and British hauteur, although somehow she had imagined the Mexicans were even more formal than the English. Or was that the Spanish?

Feeling more provincial than ever, she made her way downstairs after a hesitant look around her and found Jill.

"Think you can handle them?" the older woman asked, reclining on a wrought-iron lounge sipping something tall and frosty.

"The children, you mean? They're marvelous!"

"If you say so." Jill shrugged. "You'd think they'd never had a friend, the way they latch on to every woman who comes along. They bugged me, too, when I first came here, but they finally caught on."

"Jill!"

"Jill!" Jill mocked, gesturing to the drinks cabinet. "Honey, you've known me long enough to know that, while I may have my faults, hypocrisy isn't one of them."

"Then why did you offer to come look after them in the first place?"

"You think I should have offered to come along to warm his bed and inveigle a proposal out of him? Oh, Lucian would have gone along with that in a big way, after all the floozies trying their luck with him ever since he and Larice broke up. Before that, too, no doubt." She extended a shapely ankle and twisted it to admire the gold sandals, obviously new. "Credit me with a little more finesse, love. When I want something, I make up my mind how to get it and proceed. Simple? Or do you think it's more honorable to go around with a sanctimonious expression, taking pot luck with a yes, ma'am, thank you, ma'am?"

Hannah's thoughts flew immediately to Jill's marriage to Bill Tolland and her subsequent climb to success through his inspired photography and clever management. It's possible that Jill's mind took the same turn, for she had the grace to look slightly uncomfortable.

The two women were served dinner by a round little woman whose unlined face belied her graying hair. Carlotta was an excellent cook and she stood by with a proprietal interest as Hannah sampled each course, beginning with a clear soup with an intriguing lime flavor and ending with a confection of cream and spiced chocolate.

Almost immediately after dinner, Jill excused herself, saying she wanted to have a bath and relax with the new *Vogue*. "You'll be wanting to turn in, anyway. Traveling always slays me and you can be sure the kids will see that you don't oversleep."

Hannah was tired, though not particularly sleepy. Still, dismissed as she was, what choice had she? Carlotta and Manuel, who tended the grounds and raked the blossoms from the pool, had retired to their own apartment and the children were long settled.

With her foot on the bottom step, she heard Jill call from the matching staircase across the *sala*, "There are books in the library—the double doors over there. Feel free."

Hesitantly opening the massive doors, Hannah felt slightly guilty. She'd hate to be caught poking around alone without having even met her host. On the other hand, he wasn't much of a host, not being here to greet her. Strictly speaking, she supposed she was really Jill's guest, but all the same—

Quickly, she picked up two colorful magazines from the long refectory table and, after a wistful glance at the book-filled walls, snapped out the light and closed the doors behind her. Plenty of time to explore the riches of the library after she had gotten permission from the owner.

The magazines were in Spanish and she tried diligently for over an hour, using the rusty high school Spanish at her command, to translate. A wave of disappointment washed over her as she realized that most of the books in the well-filled library would be in that language as well. Darn! She was a voracious reader, having learned early that books could make up for so many disappointments.

When she heard the low growl of a vehicle outside the thick walls, she flung down the magazine impatiently and wandered out to the balcony overlooking the courtyard. She was sorely tempted to peep over the stairs for a glimpse of this paragon who had Jill so enthralled, but she steeled herself against her natural curiosity and gazed down on the swimming pool instead.

There was a fountain at one end and the fine spatter made the surface of the water look like hammered satin. She heard voices from below. Jill's rather high, thin one and another that sounded like chocolate over gravel. The thought brought a smile to her lips as she leaned over the rail, perfectly safe from view, since the courtyard was lighted by flambeaux placed beneath the several balconies.

Jill emerged from the *sala*, swinging around to speak to whoever was behind her— Lucian Trent, no doubt—and the chiffon caftan swung sensuously about her limbs. The white cotton sun dress had been good enough for dinner with her stepsister, but for meeting the lord and master of the castle chiffon was preferred!

Strains of music flowed from somewhere inside the *casa* and Hannah heard the baritone voice again, this time noticing the accent. It was an odd mixture of Mexican and British, not unlike that of his children, although lacking the flattened tones they had picked up on the West Coast with their mother.

"I warned you that nightlife on the island would not be very exciting," he said, coming into Hannah's view as he joined Jill by the pool.

"One dance and I'll go peacefully, Lucian," Jill laughed. She swayed closer to him and he began to move with her, his arms closing about her in a relaxed manner.

Briefly, Hannah wrestled with her conscience and lost. Besides, if she moved they might see her and that would be embarrassing for all concerned. They were at an angle below her so that she could only get a foreshortened impression of her host—taller than she would have expected, broad shoulders clad in an impeccable dinner jacket. Where could he have gone without Jill? She obviously didn't fill *all* his time, then.

They turned slowly to the music and Hannah was able to see the hand against the pastel chiffon of Jill's back. It was dark, long, particularly well formed. Hannah always noticed a man's hands. When they danced behind the tubbed palms beside the pool, she slipped away to her bedroom, switching out the bedside lamp.

Long after she slid under the linen sheet, Hannah saw in her imagination that tall, Latin-dark figure whose rich voice held a hint of amused indulgence. His features, even from the high vantage point of the balcony, were intriguing, the nose long and high arched, the cheekbones almost too well defined, and the bottom lip thin but sensuous.

In Hannah's limited experience, men like that were the stuff of dreams, and she only hoped she didn't disgrace herself in the morning when she met him by blushing or stammering like an adolescent goose! There had been more than a few occasions in the past when Jill's poise and beauty had rendered Hannah's own youthful uncertainty helplessly gauche. Jill, of course, would look on in slightly superior amusement while Hannah turned every color under the rainbow and did her best to disappear.

In the end, she need not have worried, for when she awoke it was to hear the two children babbling about Papa's having gone riding, and would she please have breakfast with them?

Sleepily, she sat up and clasped her arms around her knees. "Sounds delightful. May I get dressed first?" She saw with a feeling of amused compassion that neither Kip's nor Alice's face and hands were any too clean and Kip's shirt was buttoned up all wrong. Carlotta, of course, would be busy preparing breakfast, but Jill could have— No. Jill would *not* have—not unless she'd had a drastic change of heart. Jill was a night person, seldom coming alive until noon.

They breakfasted together in the courtyard on what Alice informed her were *huevos rancheros*, a mixture of eggs, refried beans, and a hot, tangy sauce served on a tortilla. It was a good deal more substantial than the cold cereal Hannah was used to.

"I like it lots better than porridge," Kip confided. "Papa does, too. Papa says if I eat and grow big enough, I can have a pony to ride with him when he goes out on Dore."

"That's Papa's horse, and he's big and his

real name is Conquistadore," Alice explained, hardly stumbling on the mouthful.

After thanking Carlotta, the children led Hannah off by the hand to show her their most treasured places. The housekeeper, in a mixture of Spanish and English, assured Hannah that the children were free until just before lunch time.

During the next few hours, they saw a monumental termite house, a small, crystal, deep pool called a cenote, where they told her they were allowed to play if someone was with them.

"Miss Goodge brought us here but she wouldn't let us get wet and Mrs. Tolland wouldn't even let us show her," Alice complained, looking hopefully at Hannah. Hannah had gained the impression that the absent governess was not greatly missed by either child.

They followed a rocky, winding path down to a white, coral-strewn beach where the water curled transparently at their feet. A little way down the beach, a concrete pier fingered out to where aquamarine turned to sapphire, and a gleaming white yacht bobbed at the end.

Kip tossed small bits of coral out into the water, and if either of the children had urged Hannah to go wading, she would have been hard-pressed to refuse them. It was wildly inviting, but Alice warned her that there were hidden coral and sea urchins along the shore and, further out, a bad current.

The sun was growing uncomfortable as they retraced their steps up the slight incline that led to the Casa Azul. Cozumel was almost entirely flat, as was much of the nearby Yucatán Peninsula, but here and there were rocky mounds that made the going rough.

"Now we'll show you Papa's Ix Chell," Alice said importantly.

Kip turned his wide, blue eyes on his sister and she said defensively that her papa had let her help him only yesterday. "And anyway, Hannie's a grown-up."

Doubtfully, Hannah protested. "I don't think we should—" Paying her no attention, the two children pushed open a door and entered a cool, shadowy room and Hannah, helplessly, followed them inside.

There was a dusty smell, overlaid by something pungent, and on the shelves along the wall Hannah could make out broken, lumpy-looking shapes and conglomerate rocks. Light streamed through the door behind them as well as through a partially opened door on the other side of the room, one that seemed to lead into the courtyard.

"Look, Hannie, that's Ix Chell. She's Papa's Goddess of Futility." Kip pointed to a table where an ambiguous-looking lump was clamped together.

"It's Fertility, Kip," Alice corrected, then, turning to Hannah, she explained patiently, "That makes the corn grow."

The smile that hovered on Hannah's lips was wiped away in a split instant as Kip, leaning against the table in his eagerness, toppled the statue, and they watched with an awful fascination as it struck the floor and fell into several parts.

No one spoke; no one even breathed for a long moment and then Kip's wavering voice raised a wail.

"Oh, Kippy, Papa will yell so loud," Alice warned in horrified tones. She stood there, a skinny little thing with frowsy pale pigtails and wide brown eyes, and covered her mouth with her hands.

Kip howled and darted from the room and Alice took off after him, leaving Hannah staring in consternation at the crumbling heap of shards. She knelt slowly, hoping against hope that it wasn't as bad as it looked, and picked up a tiny fragment of headdress. It was even worse—some of the pieces had been reduced to dust.

The sound of footsteps behind her almost sent her sprawling as she struggled to her feet. Still holding the small chunk of stone, she turned and immediately flinched at a blast from arctic blue eyes.

"May I ask what the devil is going on? Who are you? What are you—" He broke off, his eyes going past her to the mess on the floor, and in two swift strides he was towering over her, pinning her against the table with his intimidating size, boring into her very soul with a blaze of fury.

"Don't you know enough to stay out of places where you don't belong? This is a

private residence, not some museum open to
the stupid pawing and prying of ignorant
tourists! What you have succeeded in wrecking is one of the few remaining relics of its
kind!"

"Oh, but—"

"It did not occur to me to lock this door,
even when Mrs. Tolland told me that a relative
of hers had dropped in for an unexpected visit,
but in the short time you remain with us, you
will confine yourself to the public areas of the
casa and avoid my private quarters!"

Seething with indignation, Hannah was
speechless. There was no question of her
revealing the truth, not with poor Kip frightened to death of this terrible man, but all the
same, to imply that she was a nosy, prying
tourist, an unwelcome visitor!

"You—I—you don't have to worry, *señor!*
I'll confine myself right out of your precious
Casa Azul! I'm only sorry now I even bothered to accept your invitation! Believe me, I
wouldn't have if I'd known the sort of—of—"

Trembling with anger, she stood there,
stumped for a word harsh enough to describe
her opinion of the man who towered over her.
In the faded denim shift, she looked almost
frail, for one morning in the Caribbean sunshine had not been enough to erase the shadowy pallor of three months of illness, and her
long, graceful neck looked unequal to the task
of supporting her flung-back head with its
untidy heap of light brown hair.

"I was not aware of having issued an invitation, Miss—" Lucian Trent said quietly, his eyes not missing one single detail of her appearance. One hand came out to relieve her of the broken bit, and as if its loss deprived her of her last bit of strength, she seemed to crumple, tears of disappointment not far from the surface.

She dropped her eyes from his face and tried to edge past him, muttering as she did, "I'll be on the next plane out of here. Today, if possible—if—if not, tomorrow. Perhaps you would be good enough to recommend a hotel where I could stay tonight."

"That won't be necessary. I'm sure your cousin—is that it?—would be disappointed to have you come all this way and not visit with her for a few days."

"My stepsister," Hannah corrected dully. A cloud seemed to have covered the sun as she stepped out into the courtyard, hearing Lucian Trent closing the door behind him.

"I believe Carlotta has prepared lunch. The children will join us if you have no objections."

Amazed, she stared up at him. He had come swiftly up with her, his long, muscular legs taking one step to her two.

"Of course I don't object. How could I? And anyway, I—I don't care for any lunch, thank you."

"Nevertheless, you will not disappoint Carlotta. I will see you in fifteen minutes."

With swift strides he disappeared into the house, leaving Hannah in a turmoil of con-

flicting emotions. As she made her way numb-
ly to her room, she wondered why Jill had not
mentioned having invited her to Lucian
Trent. It was beyond enough to expect her to
stay here uninvited and even the fact that
she'd be earning her keep, as Jill had put it,
could not make up for the scathing attack she
had just suffered.

What a humiliating position to be in! Why
had Jill deceived her, and more to the point,
what could she do about it now? She had her
return fare but very little left over—nothing to
spare for a few days in a hotel and—oh, it
seemed so cruel to have to go back to winter-
time with no job, no apartment, and no prospects, ever, of being able to afford a trip like
this again. All her savings shot just for one
night in the tropics!

Lunch was uncomfortable, to put it mildly.
Both children were unnaturally quiet, darting
swift, round stares in Hannah's direction as if
to reassure themselves that she had not told
on them.

As if she could! Looking at the two small
faces, so pitifully subdued, and then at the
intimidating hauteur of the man across the
glass-topped table from her, Hannah knew
nothing could make her expose either of them
to the tirade she herself had endured.

Hannah allowed herself a small, unworthy
measure of satisfaction at the sight of Jill's
unease. Her stepsister was minus some of her
usual poise as she cast puzzled glances from

under those patently false lashes, first at Hannah and then at Lucian Trent. When the silence grew too uncomfortable, it was Jill who broke it, her voice unnaturally gay. "Isn't it marvelous how well Hannah and the two children seem to hit it off together? It will be nice for them to have someone to take them around. Of course, I'd love to do it myself, but this sun. I'd burn to a crisp!" She speared a tiny shrimp and dipped it into the lime and butter sauce. "Hannah's a country gal, though. The first time I ever saw her she was all one color—hair, eyes, and skin. I think you even had on a brown dress, sis, or was it just that you'd been out hunting arrowheads or something and brought in half the field on your skirt?"

"Dr. Maitland has lots of arrowheads and things like that," Alice said. "He's a— archoligist."

As her father corrected her pronunciation, Kip sent his sister a look of misery, and Hannah took pity on him and changed the subject. "Before I leave, I would like to go swimming. In the sea, that is." She focused her gaze somewhere over Lucian Trent's left shoulder, uncomfortably aware of those penetrating blue eyes turned coolly her way. "The children told me there are sea urchins and bad currents near here. Is there another place close by where it would be safe to swim?"

"We could go to the other side," Kip cried excitedly.

"I think we can do better than that for our

guest," Lucian replied. Possibly only Hannah was aware of the sarcasm in his voice. "Perhaps I can find time to take you to the Playa Santa Helena tomorrow."

Hannah's weak protests were drowned out as all constraint fled both children. They jumped up excitedly before catching their father's eye and resuming their seats. It was plain to Hannah that Lucian was a stern parent, if not a downright harsh one.

After lunch the children departed with Carlotta for their *siesta*. Hannah was glad for a chance to escape to her room, torn as she was with conflicting emotions. Whether or not the other two followed suit, she had no idea, but during the day or two she was forced to remain here, the less she saw of her unwilling host, the better she would like it!

As luck would have it, Hannah did not see Lucian Trent again that evening. By the time she came downstairs, he had already gone out, and she spent the rest of the afternoon playing with the children in the courtyard while Jill drifted about the pool on an air mattress. The sun had dropped to the point where it no longer threatened her porcelain complexion.

Sometime during the night, Hannah awakened with that pounding of the heart that indicates either a bad dream or a disturbance. For several minutes she lay listening in the darkness to the sound of her own pulse against the soft chorus of insects. She felt suddenly terribly alone, frighteningly aware of the fact that she was on a tiny island in an alien sea a thousand miles from home.

It came again—a whimper and then a childish wail—and she slid out of bed, not waiting to find her cotton duster. She opened Kip's door and in the dim light of the moon she saw the small figure sitting up in a large, heavily carved bed. Even as she moved quickly across the floor on bare feet, he wailed again, digging at his eyes with chubby fists.

"Kip, what is it? What's wrong, honey, don't you feel well?" Hannah gathered up the damp, overheated child and crooned to him. She was not sure whether he was asleep and still dreaming or awake and unwell, but her instincts were to comfort, and almost immediately the sobs diminished as Kip buried his wet face in her breast.

"Are you better now, precious?" she murmured, inhaling the clean boy smell of his dark, curly hair. The feeling of those childish arms clutching her so tightly had a profound effect on her and her own voice was none too steady.

"Ix Chell was going to—" The voice broke off as a formidable figure loomed over them, but it was enough to give Hannah a clue as to the trouble. Poor little guilty conscience!

"What's wrong? Kip? Miss Blanchard? I'm sure there's no need for you to remain here, and if my son awakened you, I apologize."

Even in a silken robe that was belted casually around his lean waist, Lucian Trent lost none of his authority, none of his ability to intimidate her, and Hannah felt herself tingling in every cell of her body. "It was only a bad dream," she explained, easing the small arms from around her neck as she sat up.

There were still small, choked sobs, but when his father declared that Hannah could return to her room and that he'd have Mrs. Tolland see to the boy, Kip clutched at her and wailed again. "Want Hannie! Hannie stay with me!"

"Christopher! That's enough. Miss Blanchard will want to get her sleep if we're to go to Playa Santa Helena tomorrow."

That had some effect and Hannah felt the cool night air strike her throat when Kip's tear-wet face turned away to consider the situation.

"Come now, it was only a dream. You're five years old, not a baby, are you? Good night, son." Lucian stepped back after laying a surprisingly gentle hand on his son's head and Hannah turned the damp pillow and settled the child down on it. In spite of the fact that she was acutely aware of those chill blue eyes watching every move she made, when Kip's arms reached up toward her, she could not resist his plea and she leaned down to place a quick kiss on his cheek before murmuring good night.

As she left the room, Lucian Trent was right behind her. One sinewy hand clamped down on her shoulder before she could escape and she found herself the recipient of his suspicious glare.

"It would seem, Miss Blanchard, that children are not always the discerning judges of character they are reputed to be. Propinquity may have worked well for you in the past, to your sister's sorrow, but while you're in Casa Azul will you please refrain from exercising your—charms"—the word was an open slur—"on my son. He's in a vulnerable position, as you have no doubt recognized, for a child needs a mother, but I will not have him hurt by bestowing his affections in an unsuitable direction. You will be leaving here very shortly, and until then I would appreciate it if you will restrain your—generous impulses on his behalf." The curl of his lips was unmistakable, even in the dim, nightlighted hallway. His eyes had left hers as he spoke to blaze a painful trail over her, leaving no small part of her rigid, trembling body unscathed. "Do I make myself clear?" he persisted.

In spite of the warm tropical air, Hannah felt unbelievably cold in the white batiste gown that fell from a high, embroidered yoke to skim her body and brush the tops of her bare feet. She flung back her head defiantly. Lucian's words made little sense in themselves, but his meaning was unmistakable; he held her in utmost contempt and was barely able to contend with her presence in his house. The sooner she got away from here, the better she would like it!

"D-don't worry, Señor Trent, I'll be leaving here just as soon as I can throw my clothes into a suitcase," she whispered furiously, straining against the iron-hard grasp on her shoulder.

The fingers tightened even more and when she gasped at the pain, flinching involuntarily in an effort to escape, he released her immediately. "You will stay for the few days you had planned. I'll not have either my children or your sister think I have made you unwelcome. In any case, the next flight out will not be for two days."

Stung beyond discretion now, Hannah thrust her chin forward and planted her fists aggressively on her hips, completely unaware that the action threw into relief the opalescent gleam of softly rounded hips and heaving breasts. "And it would never do for anyone to hold such an unflattering opinion of your high and mightiness, would it? Well, let me tell you something, Señor Lucian Trent, I feel sorry for your children because they're stuck with you, but *nothing* could persuade me to stay here one minute longer than necessary! I'll camp out at the airport and be on the first thing that flies out of here! As for Jill, what she sees in you I don't know—her judgment of men has never been particularly good, but this time she's hit an all-time low!"

"Oh?" There was a world of insinuation in the drawled word and Hannah bristled even more. "It was my understanding that you were in accord with your sister's taste in men, at least where her husband was concerned. Was I mistaken in that belief?"

Disconcerted, Hannah wrinkled her brow. "Bill?" What did this man know of Jill's first marriage? It didn't seem likely that she would have told him, for it was hardly politic to reveal to a prospective bridegroom that one's first husband had been stolen from one's stepsister, used as a means of reaching a goal, and then discarded in less than a year.

"Sí, sinvergüenza, Bill," Lucian repeated mockingly, "but in case you have any idea of exercising your remarkable talents on the only available male, Miss Blanchard— excluding my son—might I warn you that I'm quite immune to your particular type? An initial infection, one might say, induces permanent immunity."

Stunned, Hannah could only stare at him. Whatever she had done, or at least whatever he thought she had done by invading his privacy and wrecking his work, Hannah could not imagine she deserved such blatant insults as this. She stepped back uncertainly, her eyes still held captive by the force of his own, and declared with forced bravado, "If this is an example of the famous Mexican hospitality, I can't say I'm very impressed, but at least it makes it a lot easier to cut short my vacation plans. Good night, Señor Trent!"

"Despite the fact that I was brought up in Mexico, Miss Blanchard, both my name and my citizenship are British. Mr. Trent will suffice," Lucian Trent responded in an infuriatingly soft voice.

"Your name and your citizenship could be
Hades for all I care!" Hannah flung at him,
turning away to run down the hall to her own
room. Just before she reached the door, she
heard his laughing voice following her.

"*Buenas noches,* headlong, headstrong
Hannah!"

Chapter Two

Since her room was on the morning side of the *casa*, Hannah was awakened early by the sunshine streaming across her bed. She sat up slowly, yawning and stretching, but before she could get up her door was opened tentatively. Two small faces peered around the jamb and then Kip and Alice dashed across the floor and clambered up into bed with her.

"We thought you were never going to wake up," Alice declared.

"Yes, and can we put on our baving suits now? Carlotta says we have to wait," added Kip.

With a sigh of easy surrender, Hannah gathered the two children to her and they snuggled up as if they had done it every morning of their young lives. "If Carlotta says you must wait, then wait you must," Hannah told them, suppressing a grin at their exaggerated sighs. Only after several minutes of childish confidences did Hannah remember that episode in the middle of the night. It had been encapsulated in her mind, isolated by the hours of sleep before and afterward, and now, recalling Lucian's warning, she looked down on the two heads nestled so confidently against her.

How on earth could she reject their advances of innocent friendship? It would take a heart of granite to push them away and hold them at arm's length. Besides, the very fact that they were so eagerly affectionate to someone they hardly knew spoke volumes about the lack of love in their past.

While their father might care for them sincerely—and somehow, in spite of all, she was sure he did—he was either not a demonstrative sort or he had not spent enough time with them. Either way, it was his own fault if Kip and Alice looked elsewhere for what they needed so greatly. They were desperately hungry for a mother's love, and when Lucian Trent married again they'd have it. She could only hope he would not wait too long.

Hard on the heels of that thought came another one. Jill was first in line to become the second Mrs. Trent and Jill was about as maternal as one of Lucian's stone idols. So where did that leave these two? She looked down at the two heads, one the color of ripe wheat and one the color of ebony. In the capable hands of Miss Goodge, she supposed, and those hands were probably no warmer than they had to be.

Oh, well, the solution was not in her province, and lying here in bed cuddling the two darlings wasn't going to solve anything. At least, if they all stayed busy in a group together Lucian couldn't accuse her of courting them. He hadn't told her she was not to speak to them, after all.

"I fink we're going to the beach as soon as you put on your baving suit and then I can show you how I can swim. Can you swim, Hannie? Alice got stinged by a jello fish when we lived in California and she cried, too."

"I did not! Well, not much," the little girl protested.

Hannah shoved them out of her bed, utterly disarmed by Kip's occasional lapses into baby talk. Promising to join them for breakfast as soon as she had showered and dressed, she quickly made her bed and tried to decide what to wear swimming. Her old one-piece maillot had been three sizes too large and she had planned to buy something here but there hadn't been time. She'd have to wear shorts and a halter, she supposed. The shorts were cut-off jeans and would be heavy once they got wet, but she rammed them into her bag and tied her hair back, then, reconsidering, she braided it in one long, thick plait. At least he couldn't say she was out to vamp him in that getup!

Unfortunately, Alice's curiosity brought out the fact that she did not own a suit and Lucian would not hear of her swimming in the heavy cotton jeans.

"I keep a supply of suits on hand for guests at the pool, Miss Blanchard. You have only to select the one you wish," he told her repressively.

When she declined his offer, he accused her of being unnecessarily squeamish and told her that they would go to town first so that she could buy what she needed.

There had been little doubt of the outcome of the argument from the time that Alice, with childish eagerness, had tugged Hannah's shorts and halter from her bag, wanting to see her bathing suit to compare it with her own minuscule bikini. Hannah stomped off with ill grace to the dressing room that served the pool and pawed impatiently through the selection. Most of them would not have covered a mosquito bite, and she snatched up the only one-piece suit in the drawer, a glistening jersey thing of pale peach color.

Playa Santa Helena proved to be an all but private stretch of paradise. The powdery white sands were banded on one side by lush rustling palms and young papaya trees and on the other by a calm, aquamarine surf. It could only be the impossible condition of the road that kept visitors away. From the back of the Casa Azul property a trail twisted tortuously over the dusty coral, through the scrubby manzanillas, and past a young banana plantation.

After gathering up the children's towels,

dry clothes, and the grotesque toy Kip refused to be parted from, Hannah had clambered up into the back of the jeep. Jill, of course, had taken the front seat, and after the first few jolts Hannah braced her feet and held a wriggling child under each arm. Kip's Tandy, his precious jaguar carved from onyx in some souvenir factory, jabbed her in the thigh and she was uncomfortably aware of the thick, black hair and powerful sun-bronzed neck in front of her, unable to tear her eyes away from arms that wrestled the steering wheel with such deceptive ease—brown, sinewy arms glistening with sweat under the wiry dark hairs.

Her thoughts wandered in a direction that brought a certain tightness to her midriff and when she caught a familiar mocking blue gleam from Lucian's eyes in the rearview mirror, she could have died!

She was already beginning to lose the pallor brought on by her illness but she had not tanned yet to the extent that she could hide the quick flow of color to her face. Thrusting her chin out belligerently, she readjusted her grip on the boy who seemed determined to watch the wheels as they jolted over the rocks and stared straight out to the side, where a Medusa-like growth of cactus snaked along beside them.

"Girls first!" Alice sang out when the jeep pulled out onto the beach.

"No, me first," Kip countered, breaking free of Hannah's cramped arm.

Lucian held out a hand to assist her over the tailgate and she deliberately ignored him as she hopped out.

"The ladies may change in the shelter while the men"—he winked at his small son—"change outside."

The shelter proved to be a small one-room affair of saplings and thatch, and it was suffocatingly hot as Hannah struggled with Alice's straps. Jill wore three tiny patches of white held together by black and orange beads, and while Hannah pulled up the borrowed suit, Jill smoothed sunscreen over her face and neck and settled a broad-brimmed hat over her short hair.

"Want me to do your back for you?" Hannah offered, reaching out for the bottle of lotion.

"No, thanks."

Hannah shrugged and stepped out into the blinding sunlight. It was unusual enough to see Jill on a beach trip in the first place, but to do without protection from the sun was unheard of. Even at sixteen she had spent hours a day caring for her complexion, and Hannah, who made do with an occasional splash of moisturizer and a smear of lip gloss, had to admit it had paid off.

Lucian and the children were already in the water when Jill and Hannah emerged and Hannah didn't miss the quick frown of annoyance that marred her stepsister's lovely face.

"Why don't you run along and take over the children? Then ask Lucian to come here, will you?" Jill edged over into the shade of a coconut palm as Hannah picked her way across the hot sand to the edge of the water.

Kip saw her and flailed through the shallows toward her as Alice pleaded to be hoisted up on her father's shoulders. The water was chest deep on the boy, while it struck Lucian midthigh, emphasizing the magnificence of his glistening torso in abbreviated white trunks.

Once more Hannah felt herself coloring furiously, and to cover her confusion she dived through the shallow water, finning easily with her hands until she caught the squirming small boy and lifted him into the air, joining in his laughter.

"Papa can do Alice and you can do me, Hannie, all right?" he cried, jumping up and down in her arms.

"Shoulders, Papa, shoulders! Quick, before Kip wins!" Alice yelled.

Caught up in the childish excitement, Hannah ducked beneath the surface and brought up the slippery child, steadying him on her shoulders, and then the two children were whipping their mounts out toward deeper water. Hannah galloped awkwardly until she collapsed, tumbling the small boy into the water to catch him almost immediately.

She felt something brushing past her thigh beneath the surface and jumped back nervously, and with her unexpected burden, she lost her balance and went over backward, trying desperately to hold Kip above the surface.

Almost immediately she became entangled with something warm and hard, and when she came up choking, it was to feel a none-too-gentle grip on her hair, now floating out behind her in the loosening braid.

"Float, Kip. All right, Miss Blanchard, you're not going to drown." Lucian Trent sounded as if he were infinitely weary of pulling floundering victims from the water and Hannah struggled awkwardly to regain her feet. It didn't help at all to be just that much more off balance because of his unrelenting grip on her hair.

"If you'll just let me go," she sputtered, "I'll manage just fine! Kip—Kip?" She slanted a look around, her head still held firmly in place, and a gentle swell washed her against the solid bulk of her captor. "D-darn it, let me go!" She jerked her head, winced at the pain, then lost her balance again when he suddenly released her.

Emerging in seconds from beneath the transparent water, Hannah paused only long enough to assure herself that both children were firmly in control of their father, and she struck out for the horizon, fury endowing her unskilled crawl with a speed it had never before achieved.

She swam until she was no longer seeing red, then rolled over on her back to float, her arms crossed over her chest as she drifted up and down over the soothing motion of the small waves. She had no idea how far she had come, nor did she care. All she knew was that until she got her temper in check she couldn't go back, or she would have a few things to say to Lucian Trent that would be better left unsaid! The very nerve of the man!

Not just now, but last night—and even before that! In fact, every single time she encountered that infuriating creature she came out feeling about six inches high! Even when she had been poor, plump little Hannah, everybody's friend and nobody's sweetheart, she had held herself in higher esteem than that!

Feeling a sudden cold current, she rolled over and trod water long enough to get her bearings. She had come quite a ways from shore—so far, in fact, that at first she couldn't even see the others. Then she spotted the jeep, much further down the beach than she expected—unless Lucian had moved it for some reason. Into the shade, maybe. But no, there were the children, playing along the shore, and there was the shelter.

A chill finger of doubt touched her spine and Hannah took a tentative stroke toward the shore. It seemed to be getting further away by the minute and she had been treading water and floating for ages now, not going anywhere—at least, not under her own steam.

Just as the thought occurred to her that she was caught in a fairly strong current that was carrying her away from the shore, she saw a spot of glistening black between two flashing brown arms. Oh, not again!

She struck out for shore, cutting at an angle that would avoid an encounter with her would-be rescuer—or pursuer. From what she'd sampled so far, she couldn't be sure he'd pull her ashore if she washed up between his feet!

Her arms were beginning to flail uselessly now and her breath was a jagged pain in her side. She had no idea she was so out of shape! Distraught thoughts flickered in and out of her mind as she chopped ineffectually through the pellucid water—colder now and not nearly so clear. It had been—was it possible?—it had been a year since she had been swimming! Working weekdays and weekends as a waitress so she could go to classes five nights a week had left no time for such pursuits, and then there had been the months of illness.

She swallowed a mouthful of water and gagged, then plowed on with panic-fed determination. Just as another cold wave slapped her in the face, she felt something slide along her breast and she was rolled over onto her back.

Neither of them spoke. There was no time for words, for Hannah was beyond them at that point, and from the quick glimpse she had of Lucian's grim face, any words he cared to speak would be better left unsaid.

She gave herself up to the shuddering relief of being towed through gradually warming water, feeling his powerful legs brush across her bottom with every stroke. Her head rested on his chest, her arms dangling limply beside her, and she was aware of the strong even beat of his heart and the rasp of his breath.

After a while his motion slowed and she felt his legs sink beneath her as he turned her to him, still without releasing his hold.

"All right now?" he asked, supporting her when she would have submerged. He was obviously standing on the bottom but it was still too deep for Hannah and she floundered, trying to break away from his grip.

"Let me go." She gulped, pushing futilely against his hard, hairy chest. Her fingers tangled in something and she caught the glisten of gold amidst the matted darkness. From there, her gaze fell below the surface, past the distorted length of his body in the brief trunks, to the widespread feet, braced on the blue-white bottom. Peripherally, she caught sight of her own body and her gasp almost drowned her again. In the thin, peach-colored fabric, she might just as well have been nude. The effect on her breasts of long immersion in cold water only heightened the illusion, and when she looked up and caught the knowing expression on Lucian Trent's face, she wished he had left her to drift all the way to Tulūm!

"Traditionally, your nether regions should be scaled in silver and tipped with a fin," he murmured, lifting a drift of sodden hair from her shoulder. Somewhere she had lost the

band that held her braid and now her hair
floated around her like a swath of sargasso
weed.

"I—you—" Hannah pushed again, succeeding in freeing her upper body, only to have her
legs drift up against Lucian's thighs. Her own
heart was pounding now, even harder than
his was, although the exertion had all been on
his part.

For one fleeting instant, she thought she
saw something on the aquiline face that was
far removed from contempt, and then he
released her and stepped back, allowing her to
regain her equilibrium and swim away under
her own power.

If her old instructor at the YWCA could see
her now, she'd take back the few compliments
she had spared for her most determined pupil,
Hannah thought wryly, emerging to wade
ashore. She felt as if she weighed a ton, once
removed from the buoyant water.

The outing, she decided later, had not been
a howling success. Jill, when Hannah
dragged herself ashore, had been seated far
up on the beach in the shade of a grove of
palms, her bikini covered with a white silk
pajama suit. Under the blank stare of dark
glasses, her geranium pink lips had thinned
ominously and Hannah was reminded of
other occasions in the past when Jill had been
displeased with her.

"Thanks for delivering my message," the

older woman had gritted out. "For all you care, I could have been burned to a crisp!"

Well, how was Hannah to know Jill had been waiting for Lucian to spread sunscreen over her back and legs and who knows what else? On the other hand, it had been obvious. What other reason would she have had for refusing Hannah's offer of assistance?

Oh, well—Hannah sighed now, rolling over in bed and punching the pillow to fit the hollow of her cheek—it wouldn't be the first time she had fallen afoul of Jill's quick temper and it probably wouldn't be the last. Jill, to quote herself, was no hypocrite. If she was upset, everyone knew it and knew just exactly why.

It certainly couldn't be jealousy—far from it—for no one in his right mind could find a reason for Jill to be jealous of someone like Hannah. It was just that Jill liked to have all masculine attention directed her way, with no distractions whatsoever. Hannah, of course, would not be a distraction much longer—not that she ever really was—but the children were another matter. Jill was going to have to come to terms with the fact that Lucian Trent owed a good deal of his time and attention to his children, and no matter what Hannah thought of the man's boorishness personally, she was coming to realize that he was not a man to shirk that responsibility. In fact, his behavior today had indicated that he looked on them not so much as a responsibility but as a privilege, that he genuinely enjoyed their company.

Something inside her warmed at the thought and she went to sleep with the vague inkling of what it might be like to share in the warmth he showed his children.

Resolutely, Hannah made her plans the next morning. She finished her breakfast alone, for Lucian and the children had disappeared and Jill, of course, was not yet awake. Carlotta chattered to her in a mixture of Spanish and English and Hannah managed to catch every third word or so, making out something about Passion Isle and a boat.

She nodded and smiled, offering *gracias* for the *huevos,* and asked about a telephone. "Phone—*teléfono, comprende?*"

Carlotta beamed and nodded, gesturing to the library.

Minutes later, as Hannah heard the jeep pull up outside, she swore under her breath at the mediocrity of her language course in high school and the inefficiencies of the local phone system. She was still trying to make herself understood, and just when she thought she might be succeeding, she was treated to a spurt of rapid-fire Spanish that left her seething in frustration. She was belaboring the point—"*Aeronave*—Miami—today? *Mañana?*"—when she heard someone come into the room behind her. She cast a quick, despairing glance over her shoulder.

It was Lucian, and he mouthed the words "May I help?"

Resigned, she handed him the phone. "Would you *please* find out when the next flight leaves for Miami? It seems as if everyone at the airport who speaks English is either out to breakfast or on indefinite leave. I can't believe my accent is that bad!"

Lucian rattled something into the receiver, waited for a return burst, and firmly placed the phone back in its cradle.

"Well?" Hannah asked impatiently when he didn't speak immediately. He seemed intent on discovering whether or not there were any ill effects from her adventure the day before. At least, she could think of no other reason why his eyes should move so swiftly and efficiently over her. With her face innocent of makeup, her hair in an unglamorous braid, and wearing the faded denim shift, she didn't imagine he was stunned by her beauty.

"The flight is booked for today. I will let you know later about tomorrow's schedule. Now, if you will share with me a second cup of Carlotta's delicious coffee, I will tell you something of what the children and I have planned for your amusement."

Hannah followed him from the room; she had no choice, for his hand under her elbow was a thinly disguised coercion, but when Carlotta met them with a steaming pot of coffee, she refused politely and went to the edge of the courtyard, staring at the well-tended potted palms. She braced herself for what she had to say—that she had no intention of waiting around for another invitation to leave.

"Mr. Trent, what time will the first flight be tomorrow?"

"As I told you, Miss Blanchard, I will let you know when the time comes," he replied urbanely. "Schedules here on the island are perhaps a bit more casual than elsewhere."

With all the feelings of someone who opens a door only to be faced with a blank wall beyond it, Hannah exclaimed, "I want to go home! I want to go just as much as you want me to go and I'd appreciate it if you'd—if you'd—"

"Yes?" he prompted blandly.

She was silent. If only he'd stop playing with her, she wanted to say, yet how could she accuse him of that? What had he actually done to make her feel so much like a very small mouse being played with by a very large cat?

"Miss Blanchard, you mentioned our famous Mexican hospitality. Under rather unfortunate circumstances, I'm afraid, and I'm compelled to make amends. If your stepsister finds it in her heart to forgive you, then who am I to do less? I'd be very pleased if you'd consider *mi casa su casa* for the rest of your vacation."

In perplexed silence Hannah digested his words. If her stepsister could forgive her? Surely the failure to pass on a trivial message

was not that grave an offense. If Jill had
anticipated her lover's soothing massage with
the lotion and had been miffed because he
was too busy pulling a silly idiot ashore instead, was it anything that required a big
forgiveness scene?

"You'll stay on, then?" He interrupted her
thoughts. "The children would both like that
very much, for they've had their activities
curtailed since Miss Goodge returned to England. I had hoped to have a girl from the
village come during the day but even that fell
through, and I'm afraid Jill's sensitive skin
renders her unable to spend as much time
with the children at their play as she would
like."

A twist of amusement accompanied that
rather dry observation and Hannah wondered
suddenly just how deeply he saw beneath her
stepsister's flawless complexion. She had an
idea he was not fooled by any protestations of
maternal devotion, but then, he was not a
man to remarry just for the sake of his
children. No, Lucian Trent would be a man
who needed a woman for another reason
altogether.

"Chancanab, Chancanab, we want to go to
Chancanab!" the children chanted as they
raced across the courtyard to hurl themselves
at their father. Kip slammed his onyx jaguar
on the table as Lucian caught them up, one on
each knee, and Hannah feared for the glass
surface.

"You must learn to treat your friend Tandy

with more care, Kip, both for his sake and for the sake of the furniture," he reprimanded gently, lifting the small sculpture to frown at the chipped ear and broken tail. Hannah had learned why the child was so fond of the unlikely creature—it fitted his small hand perfectly and even Hannah enjoyed stroking the cool, smooth stone.

"Will you wish Miss Blanchard a *buenos días,* my children? One does not take a vacation from proper behavior."

"Buenos días, Hannie," they chorused unevenly. "We want to take Hannie to Chancanab, Papa. May we?" Alice continued.

"I think perhaps you are more concerned with taking Alice and Kip to Chancanab. Am I right?" he teased them.

"Hannie, too, Papa. Hannie can swim good."

"Miss Blanchard can swim *well,* Kip. Or should we say reasonably well?" Lucian broke off and looked up at Hannah with a flash of amusement. "Perhaps I may emulate my forward children and call you Hannie as well?" He pronounced it more like honey and Hannah felt herself flushing as she mumbled her consent.

"It's really Hannah, Mr. Trent."

"I think I prefer the children's version, and my name is Lucian."

"And should I emulate your forward children and call you Papa?" Hannah teased, unable to resist the playful atmosphere around the sun-drenched courtyard.

Through the children's quick laughter, she caught his wicked gaze and the one word, "Dare!"

The schedule for the next few days was soon settled, with a trip to Palancar Reef on order for the afternoon. Lucian excused himself without explanation and Carlotta took the children off to the kitchen for refreshments. When Manuel shuffled through the arched opening to the courtyard with a push broom and a basket, Hannah bid him *buenos días* and went in search of Jill.

If Mr. Trent—if Lucian thought she needed to ask forgiveness, perhaps she should seek it, but it was not as if she had deprived them of anything extraordinary. They certainly had all the time in the world for such diversions, for didn't they share the west wing? Oh, yes, Hannah had heard all about the two best bedrooms being on that side and the morning sun that would have ruined Jill's rest on the other side, but she knew Jill well enough to suspect that, had he lived in a one-room cave, she would have found an excuse to move into the cave next door.

Jill was not in a good mood. She had complaints lined up and numbered waiting for the moment when Hannah should walk through the door, and the barrage began with the episode on the beach.

"Really, Hannah, for a girl who's been swimming as long as you have, you put on a really lamentable performance! Lucian was not taken in one bit, but whàt could he do when you insisted on making a spectacle of yourself like that? I might have known you'd conveniently forget to pass on my message, but did you have to go to such lengths to call attention to yourself?"

After having spent a good many years with her stepsister, Hannah knew enough to lie low and let it roll over her. She waited for the next blast.

"And another thing—you know good and well I planned for you to take the kids off our hands and allow me some time with Lucian. Instead the four of you get together and plan all these outings. And you know very well I don't enjoy that sort of thing! Why can't *you* take them to this . . . Palancar, or whatever the place is?"

"Oh, you know about it?"

"Oh, yes, I know about it. Carlotta informed me when she brought up my tray. That grinning old fool has it against me for some reason, and I could tell by the look in her sneaky black eyes that she knew I'd hate the place and it tickled her to death!"

"Oh, Jill, Carlotta's not like that," Hannah protested. "She laughs a lot, anyway—it's just her nature. I like her."

"Oh, you would! You were always one of those tedious fools who spout off nonsense about loving all children and animals and old people! Well, that's just great by me because it weeds them out for those of us who like more stimulating company."

"Am I as bad as all that?" Hannah groaned, plopping herself down on the rose-colored silk slipper chair.

"Worse!" Jill intoned, but she was finished with her tirade, Hannah was glad to see. She went on filing her long nails but the petulance was leaving her face and she spared Hannah a slight, rueful smile. "Let's face it, doll— you're a much nicer person than I am. Law of compensations, I guess—although you don't need all that much compensation these days, do you?" Jill's eyes swept over the incongruous figure in jeans and halter sprawled out in the elegant chair. Hannah had the grace of a young colt these days instead of the clumsiness of a puppy, and when Jill mentioned that fact to her she added a warning: "Just don't get any ideas about trying out your newfound charms on Lucian. He eats little girls like you for breakfast! Lucian moves in the very highest circles, both in Mexico and in London, and when he marries again, it certainly won't be to any scruffy little country mouse like you, who's just found out she has a figure!"

She preened herself as if she already saw herself entertaining the theatrical greats or perhaps the hidalgos of the White City of Mérida, and Hannah could not suppress an impudent grin. There was an unlikely bond between the two of them, for all they were six years apart in age and a world apart in all else.

"You'd better prepare yourself, sister mine,"

she warned, "the children tell me we reach this fabulous place by boat."

"Oh, gawd!" Jill cried in exaggerated agony. On second thought, perhaps it was no exaggeration at that. Hannah remembered the time Bill had taken the two of them waterskiing at Lake Norman. Jill had wanted photos of herself on skis in a bikini and Bill was ready to lay down his life to oblige her. It had been a disastrous outing and Hannah felt a stab of pity for the woman who was determined to suffer anything to get what she wanted.

The sleek, fiberglass cabin cruiser that awaited them seemed to lift Jill's spirits, Hannah was thankful to see. She was following along with the children while Lucian led the way, burdened down with an ice chest on his shoulder and a load of diving gear, while Jill hung on to his arm, squealing at every pebble in the path.

The children were chattering as usual, but Hannah's attention was taken up by the figure in front of her: khaki pants that casually delineated lean hips and long, muscular legs, bare feet in deck shoes moving with perfect sureness over the rough trail, an open-weave black shirt that was still not as black as the raven hair that touched the collar, his shoulders and arms . . . With an odd tightening in her middle, Hannah remembered the feel of those bare muscles yesterday as he had towed her in from a deep strong current.

There were other currents, stronger and deeper, she reminded herself sternly, that could be even more dangerous. She forced her attention back to the children as Kip asked her to take Tandy so he wouldn't get sunburned. She tucked the toy into the basket Carlotta had lent her along with the towels, sweaters, and lotions. It was a charming basket, an open-topped design of colorful straw, and Hannah made a mental note to get herself one to take back as a practical souvenir.

Thinking of souvenirs brought a pang of sadness, for already she had fallen in love with the tiny, sun-drenched island and its friendly, easygoing people. Not that Lucian Trent could be numbered among the friendly, easygoing ones, she hastened to correct herself—nor had she fallen in love with him! The very idea brought a warmth to her face and she was glad everyone was too busy boarding to notice.

Palancar was a reef a mile or so offshore. As Lucian stood braced, feet apart, at the wheel, easing the sleek hull through water of incredible color and clarity, the children informed Hannah and Jill of the different types of coral and fish to be found there.

"Not for me, sweeties," Jill declared. "I'm strictly a dry-land sailor." She had arranged herself in a carefully casual pose that showed off every lovely line of her body and made certain that she was in full view of the man at the wheel.

You could say what you would about the glamour of a tan, Hannah thought wryly, but Jill's pink-white body in the black crocheted bikini made her feel like a plate of leftover French fries. It was not only the borrowed suit, the unglamorous pigtail, and the cheap rubber thongs. It was just that it was not as easy to shed the inhibitions of the past as it had been to shed the pounds that caused them.

"You know how to use a snorkel?" Lucian asked Hannah after dropping anchor in what appeared to be the middle of nowhere. He didn't even suggest that Jill might like to try, and when Hannah admitted she had once tried it in a swimming pool, he nodded and selected a mask and snorkel from the pile of equipment the children were pawing through.

The flippers were awkward and he helped ease them on her, showed her how to clear her mask, and then went over the side, instructing the children to follow him.

It was another world. Mosques and domes, branches and plumes as well as exotic formations that bore no resemblance to anything she had ever seen before—and through it all moved an incredible variety of jewellike fish, drifting in and out of the slanting beams of light like some strange, silent corps de ballet. Impossible shapes, enchanting colors, all tinted by varying shades of blue, the whole scene swaying as if to some unheard concerto.

Hannah was totally entranced. She hung there just below the surface and watched until she almost felt herself a part of the rapture, and then something grabbed her foot and tugged.

Startled, she floundered, filling her tube with water, and before she could recover her balance she was choking and struggling to escape from the unfamiliar mask and mouthpiece.

Arms came around her from the rear and she rose above the water. Then a hand slid the mouthpiece out of her mouth and lifted the mask to her forehead. She felt herself supported from the back as Lucian pulled her against his chest and slowly trod water while she regained her composure. Really, for a fair-to-middling swimmer she managed to get herself into the most ridiculous situations when he was about! No wonder Jill thought she was trying to get his attention.

Guiltily, she glanced at the hull of the boat, its white sides scintillating with dappled reflections, and breathed a sigh of relief when nobody appeared to be watching. The children were darting around like water babies, obviously perfectly at home in the water, and Hannah gave a kick, trying to disengage herself from her captor.

"It's all right," she gasped. "I've got myself in control now. It was just—you know—I couldn't breathe for a minute!" She felt his hands slide along her sides as she moved away from him, stroking and kicking all the more energetically because she was so reluctant to leave that particular shelter.

"I apologize for my children. Alice pulled your foot. She did not realize, perhaps, that you were still unaccustomed to the snorkel."

"Oh, that's all right. It's one way of getting used to it in a hurry, isn't it?" She slid the mask back down and installed the thick rubber mouthpiece and moved away, more intent on escaping from his disturbing presence than on the wonders below.

While Hannah dried off the two children and got them into fresh clothes, Jill dozed on the cushioned bench that ran along the sides of the open cabin. Hannah had insisted she take a motion sickness tablet before they left and she was glad now, for the gentle rolling would have been disastrous.

"Where's Lucian?" Jill asked drowsily.

"Papa's spearing us some fish," Kip informed her, slinging aside his tiny wet trunks to reach his toy jaguar.

Some of the spray landed on Jill's legs and she sat up with an impatient snort. "Ouch! Can't you get them out of my hair, Hannah? All this athletic junk makes me tired!"

Hannah quickly complied. Jill's idea of exercise was a night out at a disco, and the fact that Lucian seemed to prefer diving, swimming, and riding was obviously not according to her plan of action.

After raising the anchor, they cruised further until they came to a clear, sandy bottom, and once more Lucian went over the side. Hannah watched as those dark, powerful limbs propelled him deeper and deeper through the crystal clear water. With the distortion, it appeared that his muscles were rippling constantly and she chided herself for being unable to tear her eyes away from him. She had had two or three boyfriends since the ill-fated thing with Bill Tolland, and there had been the usual kisses and even a proposition by a fellow who thought that just because she wasn't a fashionable size five, she'd be grateful for any masculine attention she could get.

Even so, no man had ever had the effect that Lucian Trent had on her without even trying. Lord, if he ever found out, he'd die laughing! Worse still, if Jill discovered her stepsister's silly infatuation she'd be merciless. Jill was a predator who had staked out her territory and Hannah knew from past experience it would be worth her life to invade it.

Foolish thoughts! As if she would. As if she *could!* It must be an overdose of sun, she thought scathingly, tugging a borrowed straw hat down over her head.

"Here he comes and he's got two!" Kip sang out. Both children were hanging over the rail watching when Lucian broke the surface like some emissary of Neptune's kingdom, complete with a huge pink conch in each hand.

"Kip, let me take Tandy before you drop him overboard," Hannah said. She thought privately that an immersion wouldn't hurt the thing. It was becoming distinctly grubby since the children had been gobbling down the refreshments Carlotta had provided ever since they got back into the boat.

Hannah served the adults sandwiches and cold drinks and averted her gaze when Jill handed Lucian the lotion bottle and asked him to spread it over her shoulders—"not because I need it, darling, but just because it fe-eels so good," she drawled. Even so, she did not miss the quick look of annoyance that flickered across his face as he put down his bottle of *cervesa* after one deep draught.

They decided that because Jill had had enough of the outing, being a nonswimmer, they'd take their catch home to have Carlotta prepare it instead of going on to San Francisco Beach or Passion Isle.

"Hmmm, that last sounds intriguing, darling," Jill murmured, "but under the circumstances, maybe we'd better skip it."

Hannah had no doubt what those circumstances were and she herded the disappointed children aft, where they made noises to hear the effects of the engine's vibrations on their voices until Jill yelled at them to shut up, for heaven's sake. Hannah then promised them a special treat and spent the rest of the trip racking her brains to come up with something.

Jill elected to help Lucian steer the boat and she stood beside him, shivering deliciously as the cool breeze struck her bare body. Of course, Hannah thought sourly, she *had* to huddle close to him to keep warm! She couldn't just put on a sweater like everyone else.

By the time they reached the pier both children were all but asleep. After securing the boat, Lucian helped Jill ashore and then reached for the children, taking one in each arm as Hannah lifted them up to him.

"Can you manage alone?" he asked.

"No problem. I have to gather up the odds and ends and then I'll follow you." A soft smile lit her face as she looked at the two sleeping children, the dried salt leaving a powdery residue on their sun-kissed faces. "I'll be there in time to get them settled down."

As she watched his swift strides eat up the distance along the narrow path, a sigh escaped her, a sigh that expressed some otherwise inexpressible longing deep inside her.

Shaking herself impatiently, she gathered up the wet suits, towels, Kip's Tandy, and one tennis shoe—Lord knows where the other one was. She crammed them all into Carlotta's basket and took a quick look around her before climbing up to the rail of the boat. It had been an easy matter to get on and even easier to tumble overboard at the reef, but it felt shakier now that she was alone. The concrete pier was not more than eighteen inches away, scarcely more than the thickness of the plastic fenders, and she stood up quickly, braced herself and jumped.

Just as her feet hit the concrete she heard something plop into the water. Oh, drat!

Hastily, she checked the basket, but could find nothing missing. It was probably just a bottle of lotion anyway, and since neither she nor the children used it, Jill would have to stay indoors or do without. Or maybe Hannah would try out her diving skills in the morning. That might be fun.

As she trudged up the path, she saw the gleam of the pier light behind her as it came on in response to the gathering darkness.

The casualty was Tandy, but Hannah did not find out about it until much later, when she had gone up to her room for the night. The children had been wide awake and starving when she had reached the *casa* and she had laughed at the resiliency of the little creatures. One minute flaked out, the next raring to go!

As a special treat, the children were allowed to join the adults for dinner, which Hannah told them after a bit of swift figuring was their surprise. She didn't get away with it; *she* herself had to provide the treat, and dinner was something else. She promised an extra special story before they went to sleep and they were satisfied.

Carlotta performed magic with the fish and conch, and as Hannah polished off a second serving of *ceviche*, Lucian told her how it was prepared. She tucked away in her mind the details of the lime juice marinade, with a seasoning of olive oil, peppers, onions, and tomatoes, and mourned the lack of queen conchs in Winston-Salem.

"Then you must return to Cozumel whenever your hunger overcomes you," Lucian teased.

"Better watch it, Hannah. You'll be right back where you were at this rate," Jill gibed, then, ignoring the agonized pleading in Hannah's eyes, she turned to Lucian. "You'd never guess that our Hannah was a little butterball, would you? She used to watch me pour cream over my strawberry shortcake and practically weep, didn't you, hon?"

Lucian, perhaps more sensitive to Hannah's embarrassment than she would have given him credit for, murmured something about baby fat but Jill wouldn't let it alone; oh, no, she must elaborate.

"She wasn't really gross, you know, just pleasingly plump, as the saying goes—a real little bouncer. She used to get absolutely furious when the kids called her Hannah-ball."

Hannah could have sunk under the table. Lucian refilled her glass with the pale rosé wine and offered her the fruit bowl and Jill, piqued, perhaps, at his attentions to someone other than herself, persisted. "If I'd known she had finally worked it all off I might have thought twice about having her here. The last time I saw her she was still a roly-poly."

The look Lucian cast her way was strange, Hannah thought, almost as if he didn't believe Jill's description. "You must have worked very diligently," he remarked with a lift of those dark, slanted brows.

"No, I didn't, as a matter of fact," Hannah said grimly. "I was sick! Flu, then pneumonia. Now, may we change the subject? Please? It's not one of my better memories."

The eyebrows again. "But this is terrible! This happened recently? This perhaps explains why there were shadows in your face when you arrived that have been erased by the sun."

"If there were shadows, yes, I suppose that's the reason. It's certainly the reason I jumped at the chance when I got Jill's letter. It was sleeting for the third day in a row and I could practically smell the sunshine and flowers when I opened the envelope." Hannah looked at Jill, not missing the tightened expression on her face. "It didn't occur to me that I might take you up on it, you know, but Bill insisted. So—here I am, compliments of Bill, Rosa, and Citizen's National Bank."

Kip was practically asleep in his plate and Hannah was glad of an excuse to escape. She was far from comfortable as the subject of conversation and she gathered the small boy up and beckoned to Alice.

"Story, Hannie," he mumbled, rousing when she headed for the stairs.

"When you're in bed," she promised.

"In the hammock!"

Alice took up the plea and Hannah swerved to the other side of the courtyard and settled them resignedly into the colorful sisal hammock, one on each side of her. That put the width of the court as well as the fountain and the tubbed palms between her and the others and of that she was thankful. She could do without the oddly speculative looks of her host, and her stepsister, for some reason, had not been happy with her. Served her right for introducing the subject and calling Lucian's attention away for a few minutes.

She told the story of a little Indian brother and sister who might have lived in North Carolina five hundred years ago. Since history had been one of her favorite subjects, she had no trouble making her characters both interesting and authentic and she was so engrossed in the adventures of Morning Star and Noisy Bear that she was startled when Alice tugged at her sleeve to whisper that Kip was asleep.

"Oh. Well, in that case, why don't we make this a continued story and tonight after you're asleep, too, I'll try to remember more about our little Cherokee friends."

Only when he appeared at her side to lift the sleeping form of his son did Hannah have any idea that Lucian was anywhere near. He probably didn't trust her to tell a suitable story, she thought uncharitably as they herded the two upstairs.

Lucian left her as soon as he placed the boy on his bed and, after settling Alice, Hannah decided she had had enough for one day, too. She could still feel the motion of the boat and had that pleasant sense of well-being that comes from a day spent on the water.

Besides, she had no wish to play gooseberry. Jill in her glamorous caftan and Lucian in navy shantung slacks and crisp white *guayabera* could do without a third person in a faded sun dress. Her place was here with the children anyway, whether or not Lucian agreed, for it was Jill who had invited her and spelled out the conditions of her stay.

Feeling slightly sorry for herself as the poor stepsister, she made a rude noise at her reflection in the mirror and pulled her nightgown on over her head. Enough of that, my girl! You're here on a once-in-a-lifetime dream vacation and feeling sorry for yourself?

She had not yet gone to sleep when she heard Kip's sleepy whine. Tiptoeing into his room, she leaned over him, soothing back the hair from his damp forehead. "What is it, darling? Another dream?"

"Want Tandy," he whimpered.

Oh, Lord, she had forgotten. "Why don't we let Tandy sleep where he is tonight?" she said, hedging.

It wouldn't work; nothing would work but that she retrieve the wretched animal and only Hannah herself knew that he was at the bottom of the water under the boat.

Returning to her room, she tugged her gown off, stepped into her underpants, and pulled the shift back over her head impatiently. As she went quietly down the stairs she could

hear music coming from the *sala* and she
hated to interrupt, but Kip showed signs of
working himself up into a real state and it just
wasn't worth it.

She stood in the doorway and bit her lip in
consternation. Lucian and Jill were dancing
slowly, both Jill's arms resting over Lucian's
white-clad shoulders. Neither of them saw
her and as something painful twisted inside
her, Hannah turned away and let herself
quietly out the door. Why should she care, she
asked herself on the path down to the pier?
She had been here a few days, would probably
stay a few more, and that would be the end of
it. She'd never see him again—unless he
married Jill.

She pushed the idea out of her mind. It
didn't bear thinking about. There was something insidious about these lotus-eating lati-
tudes, with the moon tossing sequins across a
beckoning sea and the perfume of a thousand
blossoms seducing her senses.

The water was as clear as glass, with none
of the blue tint so visible during the day. She
could see each grain of sand on the bottom,
magnified by the smooth undulations of the
surface, and a fish darted into the light, and,
as if startled by her appearance on the end of
the pier, it darted out into the darkness again.

As she peeled off her shift and felt the night
air strike her body, she was glad she had not
tried to put on the damp bathing suit again.
There was no one here to see her, for the

nearest neighbor was several miles away and Jill and Lucian were certainly not concerned with anyone but each other.

It was magic! She had always wondered what it felt like to swim nude and this was almost the same. The tissue-thin nylon of her bikini pants didn't matter. She flipped over and dived to the bottom, touching the grainy surface and rolling slowly over to drift up to the surface again. It was marvelous! If it had been dark and murky she would not have dared, but this was as clear and safe as a swimming pool and she cavorted for several minutes before she remembered her mission. What if Kip woke up and cried out again? She had promised to tuck Tandy in beside him and he had dozed off trustingly.

She estimated the spot where the basket had tipped as she jumped out of the boat and took a deep breath. Pale onyx against a grayish white bottom could be tricky, and if the thing had sunk in the sand, she'd be out of luck. The shadow of the hull seemed to encroach and it made her a little nervous, but she finger-walked along the bottom until she saw the chipped ear and one angular shoulder and grabbed it quickly, surfacing just before she ran out of air.

Looking up at the sheer wall of concrete she wondered for the first time how she was going to get back up. It had been so simple getting down, but the pier must have grown in the few minutes she had been in the water. There were no handholds that she could see.

Clutching the toy in one hand, she paddled awkwardly around the end, veering out around the boat. The light was much dimmer on the far side of the hull and the water was beginning to feel chilly.

There was an inset step on the other side but it seemed awfully high up. Treading water, she measured the distance and decided that if she swam right up against the pier she could just reach it with her fingertips. But that would mean brushing up against the thick, waving growth of seaweed and crustations. She shivered and turned to face the shore. The beach along here was rough, dotted with coral rocks and the remains of an older concrete pier, and Lucian had mentioned the dangers that could hide in such waters.

Still, what choice had she? Headlong, headstrong Hannah, you've done it again!

"Give me your hand."

Her head jerked up and she saw silhouetted against the light a dreadfully familiar figure.

"Come, come quickly now, give me your hand!" Lucian ordered.

"I can't," Hannah protested, kicking frantically as she waved a hand to maintain her balance. She was excruciatingly aware that she had on practically nothing and that the light at the end of the pier revealed the smallest shell on the bottom.

Lucian knelt down and extended a hand. "Of course you can. Come now, give me your hand. I promise to raise you gently so as not to scrape your body against the sharp edge."

"Mr. Trent—Lucian, please," Hannah wailed, struggling frantically to stay afloat. Panic plus a handful of onyx seemed to rob her of all her natural buoyancy. "I—I don't have a suit on. Couldn't I just swim ashore?"

"Not unless your one article of clothes is a pair of shoes, and from where I stand that does not appear to be the case. Here, take my hand, girl."

"Move away from the light then—please?"

"I'll turn it off if that's what's troubling you, although I should not have thought undue modesty was a part of your nature."

She gasped and swallowed a mouthful of water as he switched off the night-light. Suddenly, the water seemed threatening, and when Lucian spoke impatiently to tell her that the fish that shared the waters with her at night were mainly barracuda, she yelped and started thrashing toward the pier.

He reached down and touched her wrist, instructing her on how to launch herself so that he could get a better grasp, and within seconds Hannah was caught up under the arms and hoisted dripping to the safety of the pier.

"Your skin is cold. Had you no better sense than to swim alone in strange waters?" he chided, rubbing his hands briskly up and down her back.

With her heart still pounding from the specter of carnivorous fish, Hannah tried to gasp out her reasons, but he hushed her impatiently. Still stroking her flesh, he pulled her against the warmth of his chest and she hung there, winded, wondering why her own heart was pounding as hard as his now that the ordeal was ended.

"What made you do such a childish thing? Is it that you are as your sister said, a foolish creature who disregards authority? If I had not seen you walking along the path you might now be in serious trouble."

"I dropped Tandy," she said, panting. "Earlier, when we were leaving the boat, only I didn't know it until I went upstairs later."

"And it did not occur to you to ask me to retrieve it?"

She lifted her head, seeing the dark thrust of his implacable jaw. "I—I hated to disturb you. It seemed a simple matter and—and the water wasn't cold—or even very deep."

The movement of his hands had slowed now and one of them had moved up to the back of her head. "Deep enough, *chiquita*, to be dangerous under certain circumstances. You seem prone to get in over your head, requiring my assistance. Is that why your sister refers to you as headlong Hannah?" He tilted her head now so that she could see the sardonic twist of his wide, sensuous mouth, and the moonlight seemed to be somehow caught up in his eyes, holding her in some strange sort of thralldom so that she could not tear her gaze away. "Oh, yes, your sister has told me all about you," he murmured softly.

Her mind raced frantically, telling her they were strangers, two people who had never even seen each other until a few days ago, who didn't even like each other, and yet it seemed somehow inevitable when his face blocked out the glowing darkness of the sky and his mouth came down on hers.

The kiss was only a tentative overture at first and Hannah was rigid in his arms, all her senses crying danger, but soon the potent combination of Lucian's virile magnetism and his undeniable expertise combined with the soft magic of the night and all Hannah's pitiful defenses melted away. Her lips parted at his tantalizing insistence and her breath quickened as she felt his hands on her quivering flesh, one of them rounding her hips to press her even closer to his thrusting force and the other slipping over her waist, her midriff, to cup the cool softness of her breast.

As a shaft of pure pleasure shot through her, weakening her knees alarmingly, she pushed against him, moaning a protest against the hot persuasion of his mouth.

"No, please—oh," she cried, breaking away from his kiss. He still held her and she could feel the heat of his body burning through the thin layer of his shirt that she had wet with her body. "Please, Lucian—you mustn't."

"Why not, my delightful little mermaid? Am I to have no reward for rescuing you from the deep again and again?" His lips captured hers again in a series of playful little nibbles and, in spite of herself, her traitorous arms crept over his shoulders to tangle in the thick, crisp hair that curled on his nape.

"Ahhh, *eres mucho bella, pequeña*. I begin to see what the husband of my friend Jill found so impossible to resist."

A shiver trembled over her skin and she pulled away, staring up at him through the darkness. "What do you mean?"

Tracing a line from her lips over her chin, down her throat, and into the valley between her breasts, Lucian whispered, "Is it not true that you and Jill's husband are . . . very good friends?"

"Of course it's true, but not—not the way you imply!" Hannah protested, backing away now, her arms crossed in front of her. She looked around frantically for her dress and snatched it up, turning her back to pull it over her head.

"Nevertheless, I applaud his taste—in both cases. And now with your permission I will restore the light and we'll return before a search party is sent for us." He picked up the toy jaguar and followed her along the pier. When they came to an uneven place, he reached for her arm, but Hannah pulled away and hurried on ahead, wishing she never had to enter the brightness of the house.

Her mind was in a turmoil as she searched for excuses for her behavior a few minutes ago, but there was no excuse. She had been totally abandoned, utterly shameless, and with a man she hardly knew! Not only that, a man who was all but engaged to her stepsister. No doubt Jill had told him of her previous friendship with Bill, but if he thought they

shared him after her marriage, he was very
much mistaken! A friend was one thing, a
lover quite another!

Without a word, she hurried up the stairs to
her own wing as soon as they entered the
salon. It was bad enough having Lucian's
eyes following her each step of the way, but if
she ran into Jill as well, there might be hell to
pay. Hannah was not adept at covering up her
feelings and Jill would know at a glance that
there had been more than a simple rescue out
on the end of the darkened pier. Maybe she
should have taken her chances with the barracuda!

Chapter Three

If Hannah could have found an excuse to remain in her room the next morning, she would have done so—either that or sneak out and make her way to the airport. She didn't see how on earth she was going to face Lucian Trent in the clear light of day after what had happened last night and she was not at all sure she could face Jill without guilt written across her face.

As it turned out, she needn't have worried. Alice told her that Papa and Mrs. Tolland were out for the day. They would visit friends and have lunch at the club and probably be out to dinner as well.

Carlotta's grandchild, José, was spending the day at the *casa* while his mother went to see her obstetrician. Carlotta told Hannah about her other grandchildren in the odd mixture of pidgin they had worked out between them, and from there the conversation moved to Kip and Alice and their former governess.

"Miss Goodge, she a very good teacher but not feel good for too long. Not smile for little ones. When Señor Trent come, children laugh and be noisy, *entiende usted?*"

"Have they—the children, I mean—have they been here very long?" Hannah was picking over beans and tossing the bad ones out the back door as she had seen Carlotta do.

"Oh, *sí*—Señor Lucian, he say London not good for *pobre niña* after Hollywood. *Mal*—" She thumped her ample chest. "So when Señor Morales go on cruise for *año*—year, he give *casa* to family."

Chiding herself for gossiping about her host, Hannah changed the subject. Even so, she was curious about everything connected with Lucian Trent—his first wife, his home in London, his plays. When she thought of his relationship with Jill it occurred to her that he very well might be her brother-in-law!

The shaft of dismay that shot through her was disconcerting and she stood up and handed the beans to Carlotta to wash while she went out to find the children.

It was almost ten o'clock that night before she heard Jill and Lucian come home and it was too late for her to escape. She had spent the afternoon in the pool determined to perfect her skills so that she would not have to call on anyone for help again. After the children were settled in bed, secure in the knowledge that Jill and Lucian would be dining out, she swam again and then, waterlogged, she dropped down on the lounge beside the pool to catch her breath.

It was the sound of the slamming door that aroused her—she must have been asleep and now a chill had fallen over the courtyard. She pulled the towel closer around her and felt for her sandals, and just as she was rising Jill waltzed into the courtyard and dropped into a nearby chair.

"Wheee! You should have been there, Hannah, it was fabulous! We had dinner on board the *Aegean Princess* at the captain's table and then we danced to the funniest music! Tell her, Lucian—wasn't it a scream? Can you imagine a Greek band playing mariachi? Droll!"

There had evidently been plenty of alcohol flowing. Jill's makeup was slightly blurred as if she had not been too steady when she touched it up—or as if she had lingered in the car before coming into the house, Hannah thought as she gathered up her belongings to make her getaway.

"Do you share your sister's love of dancing, Hannah?" Lucian asked.

"I—oh, well—I don't really know."

Jill laughed, the sound tinkling in shimmering accompaniment to the fountain in the pool and Lucian spared her a rather disdainful glance. "That is a rather strange answer," he remarked.

"Oh, Hannah can't stand discos and there aren't all that many places to dance back in the hills, hmmm, Hannah?" Jill jeered.

"I don't suppose I had time, really. At least, I haven't tried the discos," Hannah said. She was standing beside the lounge, ready yet somehow unwilling to leave. Perhaps it had something to do with the oddly penetrating look Lucian had given her when he arrived.

"No time for dancing? You worked at night, perhaps?"

"On weekends, yes, but I went to school weeknights, so there just hasn't been time. Yet," she amended.

"Surely this state of affairs has not lasted long. No young woman would surrender her social life, her love life so completely," Lucian said with a teasing gleam in his eye.

"Unless she happens to have a built-in social life," Jill giggled, cutting a rather malicious look at Hannah.

"I think, if you don't mind, I'll say good night," Hannah told them. Jill in this mood could be trouble and she had had enough of that.

Lucian was on his feet to escort her to the bottom of the stairs and she had no choice but to let him. Another mark against her as far as Jill was concerned, but what difference could it make? She would be leaving very shortly.

She turned to Lucian at the bottom step. "Did you find out when the next flight leaves for Miami, Mr. Trent?"

"Lucian."

Reluctantly, she repeated his name. "Lucian. Well, did you?"

Oh, those eyes of his could speak volumes and it was not flight information she was receiving either! How could he mock her this way, without ever saying a word!

"You will not be leaving just yet," he told her, and when she opened her mouth to protest he touched her lips with a finger, pressing gently and stroking their softness in a way that was unbelievably suggestive. "Hush, hush, *pequeña. Buenas noches.*"

With a sound of baffled impatience, she turned and ran up the stairs, conscious of his eyes following her scantily clad figure all the way to the top.

The children's chant of Chancanab was made clear to her the next day. Lucian strode in, still in his riding gear, just as Hannah was finishing her breakfast. She looked up from the Spanish newspaper she was struggling with to see him standing there, the sweat still gleaming on his mahogany skin and causing his white knit shirt to cling to his chest. Today he wore pale whipcord pants and high, gleaming boots, but she knew that some days he wore only jeans when he rode bareback and raced Dore through the surf. The children had told her about it and she had watched him from the safety of her balcony on more than one morning to see him stride across the grounds from the stable as if he owned the island and all upon it.

"The children tell me they wish to escort you to Chancanab today, Hannah," he informed her. "Although it occurs to me that it is they who wish to be escorted. It is not a place where they may swim alone, you understand, and I cannot always find time to take them."

"It's a beach, then," she murmured.

"To be exact, it is a cenote, a very calm, very beautiful lagoon where you may play in the water with the resident sea turtle. Does that appeal to you?"

"The livestock I have reservations about, but the lagoon sounds lovely. It appeals."

As she caught the gleam of his eyes, as if they were lighted from within, she admitted to herself that it would appeal infinitely more if he were to escort her.

"Do you ride by any chance?" he asked.

Jill wandered out into the courtyard at that moment and answered for her. "Our Hannah is a farm girl, Lucian. She rides cows and mules but I'm not sure about horses. Were there any horses on that farm of yours, Hannah?" Her voice was sweetly mocking and Hannah had no doubt of the cause; Jill had come upon the two of them together more than once in the past few days and she did not allow encroachment in what she considered her territory.

"As a matter of fact," Hannah answered her

just as sweetly, "we couldn't afford any animal that didn't pay his way, but I did manage to treat myself to a few hours on the bridle trail at Tanglewood now and then."

"Then perhaps you would enjoy riding one of my own mounts. I have a mare that should provide you with a stimulating ride without getting you in over your head—or hers," Lucian offered, the wicked glint in his eyes adding meaning to his words.

"Thanks, but I'm afraid I won't be here long enough to take you up on that," Hannah answered repressively.

"Had enough already?" Jill glanced at her with a smugly satisfied little smile as she helped herself to one of Carlotta's honey-covered pastries.

Lucian spoke before Hannah could confirm Jill's surmise. "Kip and Alice have been looking forward to an afternoon at Chancanab as well as several other outings. Since your stepsister is . . . unable to accompany them without a great deal of discomfort—and, of course, for Carlotta to do so is out of the question—I'm sure you would not be so selfish as to deprive them."

What could she say? It wasn't as if she wouldn't give an arm and a leg to stay here at the *casa* where she could see him every day, and Jill *was* unable to stay out in the sun without risking her complexion and thus her livelihood. Of course, Lucian himself could take them, she rationalized.

Reading her mind with unerring accuracy, he went on, "And I, of course, have neglected my work shamefully of late."

"Oh, are you working on another play, Lucian?" Jill asked eagerly.

"No, no, *carina*. My days as a London playwright are over, I think. It is of the plantation that I speak—that and another project that is dear to my heart."

"What do you mean *over*? Darling, you're the best! You're only beginning to climb!" Jill exclaimed, jumping up to cling to his arm as her pleading eyes searched his face for reassurance. "Oh, you're teasing!"

"No, no, *no importa*, we will talk of other things. Now, Manuel will drive you to the lagoon, Hannah, and you, Jill, will you accompany me to the club for luncheon today? I'm meeting my agent in about an hour to discuss closing out my London interests and we will be more than ready for a relaxing luncheon with a lovely lady."

Chancanab proved enchanting, its very lack of development adding to, rather than detracting from, its beauty. They left their towels and clothes on the rocky bank and slithered into the crystal water, and soon the children were squealing and splashing happily with the other children as they watched the enormous turtle's lethargic movement. Once Hannah was assured of their safety, she took a few minutes to drift face down over the seemingly bottomless caverns, their sides alive with colorful coral formations.

Manuel was quite content to sip *cervesa* with his cronies at a nearby outdoor cafe and Hannah and the children spent a long, delightful afternoon, with she as reluctant to leave as they when the time came to go.

That day seemed to set the pattern for the days to follow. Hannah had relinquished all thoughts of escape, even though she avoided examining her reasons too closely. As fond as she was of the children, as much as she loved the island, she knew it was not for these reasons alone that she stayed on.

They visited the small museum on the *zócalo* and returned twice to Chancanab, seeing little of Lucian and Jill. Deliberately, Hannah took herself away when she was not with the children, walking the beach nearby, exploring the edges of the *monte,* the junglelike growth that encroached on Manuel's carefully cleared grounds.

It did nothing for her spirits to realize that even had she remained in the *casa* she would have seen little of her host, for he seemed to spend most of his waking hours away these days. Perhaps he was avoiding her, too, embarrassed by the careless kisses he had given her that night on the pier. Hannah had tried to rationalize that episode. What man under sixty-five *wouldn't* kiss a girl he fished out of the water practically naked when she stood there like a fool in his arms and let her willingness show on her silly little face? He probably thought she'd be offended if he did *not* kiss her!

She spent hours in the pool, passing over the peach-colored one-piece suit in favor of one of the less shocking bikinis. Live dangerously, gal, you won't get many chances like this one, she advised herself, tugging the miniature patches to make them cover more of her tanned body. When she wasn't swimming or walking with the children on the beach, she was reading. The library offered a a wealth and a variety that was irresistible. Some of the books bore the name J. de A. Morales, but others were Lucian's personal property.

After an hour spent drifting on the air mattress in the moonlit pool one night, Hannah paddled reluctantly to the edge and hoisted herself up. Like Cinderella, she had a curfew, and tonight, under the spell of a full moon that played hide and seek through the clouds, she had allowed the time to pass unheeded. She dried herself off hastily, tossed the towel across her head and tucked the ends under and padded along to the library. She had dipped into the Stephens volumes that concerned the Yucatán area and now she selected Morley's *Introduction to the Study of Maya Hieroglyphs*. The fact that these were Lucian's personal books was not solely responsible for her interest; it was a fascinating subject.

She was halfway across the *sala* when the
door opened to admit Lucian and Jill and she
froze, acutely conscious of her near naked
body. Not that Jill didn't wear far more outrageous costumes, but Hannah, unlike Jill, was
not in the habit of displaying herself quite so
openly.

Smiling stiffly as she edged closer to the
stairs, she asked if they had had a nice
evening. Jill's thin lips should have tipped her
off that it had not been all that successful.

"Looks like you're making yourself at
home," she snapped, her derisive stare making Hannah feel like running for cover.

"We had a delightful evening, thank you.
We visited old friends of my father's. And you?
Have you found something to entertain you?"
After one fleeting sweep of flamelike eyes, he
had gazed as calmly into her face as if she
were wearing a burnoose, but she knew he
had missed nothing.

In her embarrassment, she held out the
book and stammered that she had made free
use of his library. Her heel struck the bottom
step and she turned to escape.

"You are more than welcome to anything
you care to borrow. May I see what you have
selected?" He held his hand out for her book
and Hannah, looking over her shoulders,
murmured something about being cold and
hurried up the stairs. She could feel Lucian's
gaze following her and that was far more
disconcerting than Jill's derisive comment
about making herself at home.

Far too restless to go to bed, she showered and slipped on her nightgown and wandered onto the outside balcony to stare unseeingly over the *monte* and the sea beyond. Shaking herself out of the daze she was in, she focused on one gently waving palm tree, taller than the rest, that was silhouetted against the moon-bright water. It was no wonder she couldn't settle down—palm trees, tropic air, the fragrance of unseen exotic flowers—and somewhere in the *casa* a man whose flame-blue gaze had the power to sear her very soul!

With no warning, the door behind her opened and Jill strolled in to lean against the carved highboy. "Exactly how long are you planning to stay?" she asked point-blank.

Hannah remained where she was. "Why?" she parried. "Do you want me to go?"

"Oh, hell, I don't know! I wish I knew what went on in that man's head!" She flung herself away from the highboy to drop down on the bed, carelessly flipping through the pages of the book Hannah had left on her bedside table. "Trying to make points?" she asked nastily.

"I don't know what you mean."

"I bet you don't. It won't help, you know. Oh, don't think I haven't seen the way you light up like a neon sign whenever he deigns to notice you, but let's face it, Hannah-ball—I'm in the choice position. I'm better looking than you'll ever be, if you lose fifty pounds, and what's more, I'm comfortable in Lucian's natural habitat. I can meet his friends on their own level." She lighted up a cigarette and blew a stream of smoke up toward the ceiling. "You, on the other hand, are a little hick from the backwoods who can't even put on a bikini without feeling like you'd wandered downtown in your underwear. No class. You just don't have what it takes, so why don't you just cut your losses and go home. You'll get over it, you know. Hearts can take a lot more punishment than you think."

"Whew! You don't leave me much choice, do you?" Hannah said shakily.

"Well, what did you expect? You've been here for two weeks already and when the baby sitter starts panting after the boss, it's time to go. It gets pretty embarrassing, you know. He doesn't quite know what to do with you—I mean, you're not exactly a guest, but then you aren't a paid employee either."

"Neither flesh nor fowl nor good red herring," Hannah quoted bitterly. "Did Lucian ask you to speak to me?"

Something flickered in Jill's pale blue eyes as she hesitated but when she spoke it was to deny the charge. "No, he'd probably put up with you indefinitely on my account, but I can't ask too much of him. Not yet, at least."

"No, well . . . I'll get out as quickly as I can. Before the weekend, at any rate."

There was an oppressiveness in the air that threatened a storm. Perhaps that was the reason Hannah awoke too early. She had tossed during the night until the bed was destroyed and every wrinkle of the linen sheets was firmly impressed into her skin.

It was barely daylight but she couldn't remain in bed another minute. Flinging back the top sheet, she swung out of bed and pulled her crumpled gown over her head.

Within minutes she had showered quietly and slipped on one of her three shifts, and then she tiptoed downstairs and let herself out just as the dawn was beginning to pearl the sky.

There was utter stillness. Not a bird sang, not an insect stirred as she followed the winding path that led to the water. She had just reached the clearing on the beach and paused when she became aware of movement; the boat rocked slightly although the sea was glassy calm, and even as she stared, puzzled, she saw a familiar figure step out of the cabin into the cockpit and jump lightly up onto the pier.

Irresolute, she stood there, one part of her, the reasoning part, wanting to escape before he saw her. Something else, though, something warm and silent that unfurled in the pit of her stomach and made itself felt along her spine, urged her to walk on down to the water and meet him. Dare she confront him here in the stillness on the very pier where not too long ago he . . .

Common sense took command and she turned swiftly to retrace her steps. She had gone only a few feet, however, when she froze, one hand flying up to choke off a scream.

Almost before her heart could resume its beating, she heard Lucian come up behind her, his hands catching her shoulders as he demanded, "*Qué pasa*? Hannah? What is it?"

She could only point. No sound made its way past the constriction in her throat.

Dimly, she was aware of the tension leaving his hands as she heard his soft laughter begin. "It's only an iguana, *pequeña*. Hideous, I'll grant you, but completely harmless. There, see? He's far more frightened of you than you are of him." He gestured and the ugly thing loped awkwardly away, disappearing into the dusty growth beside the trail.

"I—I wouldn't bet on that," Hannah whispered shakily, slightly ashamed of her overreaction.

"And I thought you were afraid of nothing, *pobre niña*," Lucian teased.

"Spiders I can take, but reptiles simply paralyze me. Always have, ever since I explored a little cave once when I was a child on a dare and it turned out to be winter quarters for a big family of copperheads." She shuddered again at the horrible memory and tried desperately to change the subject as Lucian's arm tightened across her shoulder. "I—uh—it looks as if it's going to be hot today, doesn't it?"

He grinned with the sort of gentle understanding she had seen him offer his children. "I'm afraid we may be in for a storm later on.

I thought I'd better secure the boat just in case. And you?"

"Me?" she responded, puzzled. "Oh—what was I doing." She shrugged her shoulders, uncomfortably aware of the warmth that was emanating from that healthy, vital body so close to hers. "I woke up and couldn't get back to sleep, so I thought I'd walk along the beach."

"I have a better idea. Can you slip back inside and put on your jeans? The sun will be rising in about twenty minutes and it will turn the water to gold. We'll ride along to the point and have a perfect view."

The little mare was a sorrel and Lucian told her they were a match. "Her name is Mixta"—he pronounced it in the Spanish way—"and she is related to the barbs, those tough, wiry little horses the Moors brought to Spain. Thanks to a strong strain of Arab, little ladies like my Mixta thrive on the rugged terrain."

"What about your Dore? He looks as if he'd be a handful, given half a chance," Hannah said, walking Mixta behind the tall roan. The narrow trail precluded a faster pace at the moment and she was glad of an opportunity to accustom herself to the little mare, who was showing signs of having a mind of her own.

"Dore came with me from England. He's strictly a green grass laddie, but I have hopes of producing something from him that will acclimatize well to this area."

Suddenly they came out of the almost tunnellike growth to a blindingly white beach, littered with stiff brown palm fronds, gray husks of coconut, and glistening mounds of sargasso weed. There were only a few out-croppings of coral and the flat stretch was an irresistible invitation to the two mounts.

Hannah followed Lucian's lead, her sturdy little mare making up in stamina what she lacked in stride, and she was laughing with the heady excitement of it all when she rounded the point to see Lucian tying Dore's reins to a fallen palm.

Wordlessly, he reached up for her and she slid into his waiting arms, acutely conscious of every muscle of his body as she slithered down against him. He put her away and took Mixta's reins to tie her off to a nearby tree and then, taking Hannah's arm, propelled her closer to the edge of the breaking surf.

"The sun will come up just there, behind that low line of clouds. Do you see the silver lining?" He pointed and she followed the line of his well-shaped arm, far more aware of his nearness than of the coming spectacle.

"You were right," she breathed after a few minutes. "It was well worth coming out here for."

"I promised you gold, *chiquita*, but I'm afraid I could only produce copper. Strictly a red-sky-in-morning affair today, I'm afraid."

"Sailor take warning?"

He grinned and clapped her on the shoul-der, turning them away. "Come, *niña*, while we're here I'll show you something rather special."

Silently, Hannah followed him a short way into the dense *monte*. There was a scurrying that made her glad of his nearness and then she caught sight of something the size of a large cat that stared at her curiously.

Lucian followed her gaze and laughed easily. "Coati," he told her. "Rather an engaging little chap, but I wouldn't advise you to risk a finger getting better acquainted."

"He looks like a cross between a raccoon and an anteater," Hannah ventured, watching as the animal approached them cautiously, sampling the air with his twitching nose.

"An apt description. Termites rather than ants, I believe. Come, this was not what I had in mind." He took her arm and urged her forward.

They came upon it quite suddenly and Hannah caught her breath. "Oh, Lucian, what is it?"

"It was once a small temple, to the best of my knowledge, although considering the placement of this and similar ruins, one might almost suspect them to be the equivalents of our present-day Coast Guard stations."

Hannah knelt and touched one of the rough gray stones that formed a perfect rectangle, divided into two equal compartments. It was almost leveled, with most of the stones half buried, but in places the wall rose to a height of three or four feet, high enough for the small openings facing the sea to be easily discernible.

"There are more?" she asked almost reverently.

"Yes, many more, some of them much more impressive than this, but they are not all easy to reach." Lucian stood well back, arms folded over a chest that gleamed like bronze through the opening of his shirt. His expression was unreadable and Hannah was oddly reluctant to voice her interest, remembering Jill's comment about making points. Still, she could not hold back a wistful sigh.

"It is not a comfortable trip laid on for the average tourist. El Reale, Aquada Grande— they require many miles of driving over almost impassable roads, as do some of the less spectacular ruins," he told her. Those piercing blue eyes seemed determined to fathom the depth of her interest and their cool scrutiny triggered her touchy pride.

"Don't worry, I won't ask for your time. I'm sure someone, Manuel, perhaps, will be glad to tell me how I can reach them." She turned away, head flung back proudly, and looked for the almost imperceptible path they had trod through the bushes.

Unfortunately, Lucian stood squarely in her way and she quailed at the thought of stepping into undergrowth that could hold heaven knows what terrors. Nor did he seem inclined to give way.

"If you'll lead on," she mumbled stiffly, "I think we should be getting back. The—the children will be waking soon."

"So?"

Aggravated, she stomped her foot, a futile gesture in the soft sand. "Please let me pass!"

"And if I don't, *mi pajarita*?"

"Don't call me names! What do you want from me?" she cried in vexation.

"I'm not quite certain, *mi tizón,* my little firebrand. Not at all certain," he said, surveying her insolently in a manner that baffled her and brought her blood to a rapid boil. She tried to brush past him only to be caught and swung up against the hard barrier of his body.

"Perhaps a bit of experimentation might reveal to us both what it is that I want from you, hmmm?" he murmured maddeningly. "Shall we see? Perhaps I want what your *enamorado,* Señor Tolland, wanted."

Before she could voice her outrage his mouth captured hers in a hard, punishing kiss, his arms tightening around her to render her angry resistance futile. She twisted, struggled to escape as his mouth ground insultingly into hers, and as she grew weaker and weaker, one of his hands came up to clasp the back of her head. Only then, when she was helpless against his marauding mouth, did his kiss change subtly to a gentle seduction.

Of their own volition her arms fluttered up to his shoulders, slipped around his neck, and as if from a great distance, she heard her own whimpering protests as one large, hard hand closed over the throbbing softness of her breast.

"You're contagious, *amorcita*," Lucian whispered roughly against her ear. "I tried staying away and still you do not leave me in peace."

"Please, Lucian—you mustn't," Hannah protested weakly as she felt his hand slip up under her shirt. His thumb, as it brushed again and again over the hardened nipple, sent tumultuous signals to the pit of her stomach.

"You can't hide it any more than I can, *amorcita*," he whispered against her mouth, "but we will wait. I've passed the age when I prefer a sandy beach to a smooth bed, no matter how pressing the temptation. I would not care to see mosquitos leave their brand on that delectable body of yours, hmmm?" He pressed her hips once more to his own, deliberately letting her know the state of his desire for her. "Waiting only sharpens the appetite, *amada*, when one knows the waiting will soon come to an end."

"You'll wait till Hell freezes over!" Hannah blazed at him, struggling to control her breathing and to overcome the baffling desire to weep. She charged past him, hearing the laughter rumble after her like the thunder of some wicked god.

By the time she reached the *casa*, she had calmed down enough to greet Manuel with a degree of equanimity, and when he offered to tend to the mare for her, she gratefully allowed him to lead her away. All she wanted to do was to escape before Lucian returned.

Standing under the cooling shower minutes later, she let the water stream over her as if it would wash away the pain Lucian had inflicted on her with his lovemaking. Oh, she could not deny that he had been right—she had wanted him, wanted him more than she had thought possible. Nothing in her experience had ever led her to believe that her own body could play her traitor in such a way, and to make it worse, infinitely worse, there had been something insulting in the way he assumed that she was his for the taking. It was as if he thought Hannah was available for a casual sexual encounter, an affair that had nothing at all to do with his disapproval of her as a person. Certainly nothing that would endanger his serious plans for the future with Jill.

She scrubbed herself furiously with the Loofa as tears mingled with the shower on her upturned face, and by the time she had rubbed her body to a glowing dryness and dressed again, she had put her hurt behind a wall and closed the door. It was not the first time. Behind that same wall were the subtle and not-so-subtle rejections of her childhood, from the look of disappointment in her own father's eye when he compared his chubby, plain little girl to the doll-like prettiness of someone else's child to her mother's exasperation at trying to turn a roly-poly tomboy into a daughter she could be proud of.

Hannah-ball was gone but the specter remained. Ironic, wasn't it, she asked herself, that she should be vulnerable to quite another sort of insult now that she could boast the same concavities and convexities that had made her stepsister so popular.

Just as she was about to leave her room, the children padded in, their clothes awry as usual when they dressed themselves without her aid. She straightened them out and the three of them went downstairs to breakfast. There was a certain sense of unreality about being at the table while Carlotta served the first coffee of the day. So much had happened to her before anyone else in the household was even awake! Except Lucian, of course. Oh, yes, except for Lucian Trent!

For the second day in a row, her stepsister was awake before eleven. Looking none too cheerful, Jill crossed the courtyard and dropped into a seat just as Lucian joined them from another direction. Hannah busied herself cutting through the tortilla-based *huevos* for the children, leaving any conversation to the others. She had not been able to bring herself to look up since Lucian had taken his place in the largest of the wrought-iron chairs.

"Since the Maitlands are coming for cocktails this evening, I asked those two we met

last night at the Plaza," Jill told Lucian as she
laced her Mexican coffee with thick cream.

"Oh? Would you care for some papaya,
Hannah? No?" he offered, just as if he hadn't
been with her on the beach less than an hour
ago. Turning back to Jill, he said, "I don't
imagine the young Keiths will have much in
common with Dr. and Mrs. Maitland."

"Thank heaven! That's why I asked them.
Honestly, Lucian, Mark Maitland is as dry as
old bones and that wife of his is even worse!"

Without even looking up, Hannah was
aware of the slight coolness emanating from
Lucian. She thought Jill was being dangerously foolish, for even to Hannah it was
obvious that the Maitlands were special
friends of Lucian's. Still, it was none of her
concern.

The children occupied her time for the next
few hours, and it was when she was leading
them out the back way toward the beach after
their nap that she encountered Lucian. He
was emerging from his workshop, to Hannah's acute embarrassment. She had not
gone near the place since that unfortunate
first meeting.

"You're not leaving?" he asked.

"We're going to walk as far as the big
rocks," she told him, referring to a formation
of coral that the children liked to climb on.

"We're collecting sea beans, Papa. Hannie's
going to tell us a story for every one we find."

"Then tomorrow you must hunt very dili-

gently, Kip. However, now you must excuse
Hannie. Perhaps you and Alice would like to
come and visit with Dr. Mark and Mrs. Alma
later on."

The boy looked cloudy and Alice was plainly
disappointed, but neither child would dream
of arguing with their father. Of high spirits
they had more than their share, but the
discipline instilled in them by their English
nanny was still in effect.

Only Hannah rebelled, and she was in an
awkward position, for she could not encour-
age the children to disobey their father. "I'll
see that they're downstairs whenever you
want them," she agreed flatly, trying to disguise her feelings.

"Nonsense! You'll be with my guests. Carlotta will make these sprouts presentable and
bring them down at the proper time."

"Carlotta will have her hands full in the
kitchen unless you have someone to help
her."

Lucian's eyes narrowed dangerously.
"Leave the ordering of my household to me,
por favor. You will be dressed and downstairs
at five thirty."

On the point of crowing triumphantly that
she had no suitable clothes, she clamped her
lips shut. There was no point in arguing with
him now. When the time came, she would
simply remain up in her room. By that time,
Lucian would be too busy with his guests to do
anything about it. She flounced off, a child

hanging to each hand, and promised them a full day of hunting on the beach tomorrow, all thoughts of leaving momentarily forgotten.

Hannah was in her room working on a project she had started for the children when Jill walked in unannounced.

"Look, Hannah, you will keep the kids up here for the next few hours, won't you? This is the first time we've done any entertaining since we've been here and I'd like everything to go off without a hitch."

Hannah clipped off a wild fiber and glanced up, her eyes widening in admiration. "You look scrumptious! Lucian wants the two children dressed and presented after everyone gets here, though. Sorry."

"Great Scott, why? A cocktail party is no place for them and I'm amazed that he'd even consider it!" Her good looks in the elegant gray tissue silk were marred just for a moment by the thin-lipped expression of irritation.

Hannah shrugged, working loose another section of fibers from the chunk of coconut husk. "Just passing on orders. I don't think he considers it a cocktail party, though. The Maitlands seem to be old friends of the family."

"Old is right! Dull as mud, too, but the Keiths—they're brother and sister, by the way—are something else. They're going on to the Windwards from here on one of those swinging sailboat cruises. Wouldn't I love to get Lucian away on something like that, away from those brats and that stupid dustbin he holes up in to glue bits of rock together."

"If you think that's likely," Hannah jeered, "you know a different Lucian from the one I've seen." Then, seeing the sudden narrowing of Jill's eyes, she hurried on to compliment her on the figure-hugging sheath.

"D'you really like it? I thought it might be too subdued."

"It makes your skin look like pure pearl," Hannah observed truthfully and not a little enviously.

"Thanks, doll. You'll be staying up here, I guess." Her cool glance swept the large closet where Hannah's three dresses reposed. "Of course, I *could* lend you a caftan, but you'd feel out of place anyway. The Maitlands, dull as they are, are top drawer, and Ted and Sylvia are not your sort at all. Besides, I'm sure Lucian wouldn't expect you to join us."

That's what you think, Hannah mocked silently, still not too sure she'd be able to get away with remaining in her room. "I'd like to finish these. Remember the corn-shuck dolls I had when I was young? I thought Kip and Alice might like something like them and the coconut fibers work pretty well, don't you think?"

"Sort of a goodbye gift?"

"Mmmm-hmmm. I wanted something special for them and I haven't been shopping since I got here."

"You're leaving soon, then?" Jill asked.

"Day after tomorrow if I can get reservations," Hannah replied.

Jill seemed to relax as a smile warmed her features. "Well, it's been a break for you, at least. You look loads better than when you came—shadows all gone and a great out-of-season tan."

After Jill had gone, Hannah slipped down to the kitchen to see if she could help Carlotta. She helped arrange a tray of surprisingly attractive canapés and rolled thin cheese logs in cayenne and sesame seeds before the older woman shooed her upstairs to get ready for the party.

She went, nibbling on a tiny wafer topped with minced shrimp, not bothering to argue. Kip and Alice had already had their baths and were playing quietly in a corner of the large kitchen, so there was nothing more to do. She called out a promise to help with the clearing up afterward as she climbed the back stairway and grinned as Carlotta broke into a rapid burst of Spanish.

Propping her feet up on the balcony railing after her bath, Hannah tried to concentrate on the esoteric Le Plongeon, but her mind kept straying to the soft, convivial murmur down below. Besides, it was too dark to read. Clouds had built up and now hung oppressively over the island as thunder rumbled from somewhere in the vicinity of the mainland. It was not the rainy season but Manuel had told her that, even so, they sometimes had a stormy session that could last anywhere from a few minutes to a week.

Behind her in the darkened room, the door opened and Lucian entered without bothering to knock. Peering over her shoulder, Hannah almost lost her balance and it was with lightninglike rapidity that Lucian was able to grab her chair before it toppled.

"You are late, Hannah."

"I'm not coming down. I told you that," she replied adamantly.

"You were told to be ready at five thirty. It is now almost seven. I will not have you neglecting my guests in this manner."

She stood up, regretting her bare feet and the limp blue dress as she faced Lucian, tall and bronzed and infinitely attractive in the white pants and *guayabera*. "They're not my guests and I'm under no obligation to entertain them," she said stubbornly.

Sparks shot from beneath his lowered lids. "Nevertheless, you owe it to me, as your host, to oblige me in this matter. I will give you five minutes to change into something suitable."

Futile anger washed over her. "Lucian, if I *had* something suitable, maybe I'd have agreed in the first place! I brought exactly three dresses with me and you've seen those. I don't think your friends would appreciate my thrift-shop originals!"

"Don't be such a little snob. Clothes are *no importa*."

"Ha! Then why didn't you let Kip and Alice stay in their shorts and sneakers? Why did Jill see fit to wear silk?" she demanded, her voice growing a little uneven as she flared up at him. Something was driving her to fling taunts at him, and if he didn't leave her alone she might say something disastrous—if anything she could say would ruffle that implacable facade. The quintessential male, leaning indolently against her bedroom wall making her totally aware of her feminine vulnerability with a mere flick of those slashing brows. It was as if they were communicating on two different levels at once and the words they spoke were only meaningless sounds.

"Wear the yellow dress," he told her softly, bringing his shoulders away from the wall. "The Maitlands are old friends of my parents and I'd like you to meet them. Besides, my voluble children have been prefacing every sentence with 'Hannie said' and 'Hannie thinks . . .' Mark and Alma are beginning to suspect I'm hiding the Delphic Oracle."

She blinked once as the tension drained from her shoulders. She must have imagined it all, that subliminal feeling of excitement that had thrummed through the atmosphere a second ago.

"All right, if you insist. The children must be getting tired anyway, so if I stay for a few minutes, I can bring them up and get them settled."

"We'll see" was all he said before closing the door quietly behind him.

Chapter Four

As soon as Lucian had left her, Hannah slipped the buttercup linen over her head, noting with a certain satisfaction that its plain, high neckline and square-cut armholes made the most of her tan. With the Grecian sandals and her hair piled into a loose knot on her head, she looked cool and neat, at least, she decided. And after all, what difference did it make? She'd never see any of these people again. She pushed away the knowledge that only one man's opinion mattered—Lucian's.

Sylvia and Ted Keith were with Jill in the courtyard when Hannah came downstairs, so she was spared their critical appraisal. She was introduced to Dr. and Mrs. Maitland, who immediately put her at ease. It was impossible to stand on ceremony when children were

concerned, and the children were very much
concerned at the moment. Kip slithered down
from Dr. Maitland's lap as soon as Hannah
settled on the couch and climbed up beside
her to announce that he was going to get a
pony of his very own.

"On your next birthday, Christopher," Dr.
Maitland reminded. He went on to explain
that his own grandson in Mérida had out-
grown his pony and now needed the space to
stable a larger mount.

When Kip dashed out into the courtyard to
tell Jill and the Keiths his big news, Alice took
his place and confided that she was to have a
piano for her birthday, and the conversation
turned to music in general.

Just as Lucian brought Hannah a tall, cool
drink, Kip wandered back, looking somewhat
subdued.

"And what did Mrs. Tolland have to say
about your good news, son?" Dr. Maitland
asked indulgently.

"She said, 'not now' and to 'run along,'" the
small boy replied dolefully.

Hannah caught the lift of eyebrows ex-
changed between the Maitlands and Mark
Maitland tactfully changed the subject. "Has
Lucian shown you any of our ruins yet, Miss
Blanchard?"

"Oh, are you interested in archaeology?"
Alma chimed in.

Jill, who strolled into the *sala* to refresh her
tequila at that moment, answered before
Hannah could speak for herself. "Oh, Han-

nah's been cramming madly ever since she discovered Lucian's passion for old rock heaps. I daresay she never heard of a Mayan until he mentioned something about the ruins on the *casa* property."

There was an uncomfortable silence and Hannah felt her face grow warm. Even the younger couple, who had followed Jill inside, seemed slightly embarrassed at her tactless remark. It was Alice, however, who broke the silence. "Yes, she had, too, because Kippy and I told her all about them that first day when Kippy broke Papa's . . ." Her piping voice trailed off as realization crept over her and Hannah followed her stricken gaze to Kip's anguished face.

"The children have taken me to Chancanab several times," Hannah exclaimed brightly, determined to steer the discussion away from the child's misdemeanor. "Kip wants to hitch a ride on the turtle's tail, but I'm afraid to let him get that close. Can a turtle harm you? Do they bite?"

The talk resumed on a more comfortable level and from turtles it moved to real estate, banana crops, and the henequen plantation Lucian owned on the mainland.

At a convenient moment, Hannah said good night and herded the children upstairs. They had eaten an early supper and since the others were considering dining at the Keiths' hotel, she decided it would avoid awkwardness if she left first. She had settled the children and was considering bringing a sandwich upstairs and reading in bed when her door burst open and Lucian strode in to glare at her from glacial eyes.

"Why do you continually use my children as an excuse to escape me? Carlotta could have taken them upstairs."

"And why do you continually barge into my room without even bothering to knock?" she countered angrily.

"You would have admitted me?" he asked silkily.

"Of course not! That's not the point anyway. I—I could have been dressing or—" Arms crossed defensively across her chest, Hannah turned her back on him. The room seemed to have shrunk enormously all of a sudden.

"Perhaps my luck will improve the next time."

She turned to glare at him. "I heard the others leave. Why aren't you with them?" she demanded.

He shrugged. "Another noisy restaurant, another poorly prepared meal. Why should I subject myself to that?"

"They're your guests, that's why!"

"As are you. Will you join me at the restaurant, then?"

"I'm Jill's guest!" she corrected. "Yours, too, in a way, but that's not important. I came to look after the children, not to be entertained by you or anyone else!" There, let's set the record straight once and for all, her belligerent expression said.

"Your sister is inclined to be . . . mischievous, shall we say? She allowed me to believe that her young relative had dropped in unexpectedly to avail herself of the opportunity of a free vacation. All very embarrassing, of course, but understandable in one so . . ." He gestured helplessly with his well-kept hands and Hannah had no trouble filling in the rest. Jill had never ceased to consider the Blanchards hopelessly countrified, even though both Hannah's parents had been university graduates.

"Just because I was born on a tobacco farm, there's no reason to think I can't discuss anything but priming and tipping," she said defensively. "Jill *did* ask me and I'm sorry if it wasn't convenient. I did try to leave, you know. In fact I've tried several times—every time you told me I wasn't welcome here!" She glared at him accusingly and Lucian had the grace to look uncomfortable.

"It seems I owe you a large apology, *pequeña*, but first, you yourself must apologize for allowing me to believe what I did of you. You put me in an intolerable position, Hannah. *Dios!* Did you really think I would have beat my son for breaking the Ix Chell?"

She glanced at him quickly, then away again. "I—I didn't know you then. Not that I know you any better now, but you seemed so—"

His low laughter startled her and she met those mocking eyes. "Come, *mi pajarita*,

surely you know me somewhat better by now?
What must I do to better our acquaintance
then, hmmmm?"

"I'm not talking about that!" she whispered
furiously. "And besides, I wish you would stop
calling me names! You know I don't know
what you're talking about."

"Mi pajarita? My little bird? But then, you
are very like a small brown bird, are you not?
You hide against the background of the forest,
and when someone comes too close you fly
away, revealing startling flashes of loveliness
that might be overlooked by the casual observer."

In spite of herself, Hannah glowed at his
indulgent tones. Bill had called her a wren
once, but Lucian hinted at something more
exotic, more . . . Stop it! she charged herself.
The man could talk the birds down out of the
trees, but that doesn't make him any less
dangerous. "All right," she conceded, "maybe
we're even now, and as much as I've enjoyed
my stay, I really do have to be leaving, so if
you don't mind—" She looked at him anxiously.

"Perhaps I have maligned the airlines
enough," he told her with a smile that shafted
right through her. "Would you consider remaining, Hannah? Jill tells me you have no
job and that you are presently staying with—a
friend. Would you not enjoy looking after my
children and living here at the *casa* with us on
a more or less permanent basis?"

Warning bells sounded. She wanted to say

yes, please! She wanted it too much and that was why it would be better to say no, to leave now while she could still call her soul her own.

"Hannah . . . perhaps it is not my right to speak of such things but you are a young girl, you have no parents to guide you. Would it not be best to . . . give up this life you have embarked upon, to prepare yourself for the day when you will meet a decent young man who will want to make you his wife?"

A frown slowly gathered on her smooth, tan brow. "I'm not sure I know what you mean."

Impatiently, Lucian shrugged away from the wall where he had been leaning to pace the floor. "Look, *chiquita*, your sister has told me about Bill. I'm not judging—you are very young, and perhaps being left alone made you more vulnerable, but it must end. It . . ."

"Just a darn minute, Lucian Trent, what are you insinuating? I've heard your little digs before and told myself I must have been mistaken, but maybe I wasn't! Just what has my charming stepsister told you about me and her ex-husband anyway?" She faced him like a small fury, cheeks and eyes blazing even as she felt something sinking inside her.

"Are you denying it? Are you telling me that you did not take advantage of the time when your sister was in New York to ingratiate yourself with her husband? Are you not living with him even now? Ahhh, come, *chiquita*, I told you I am not blaming you for these things. Even I find you very difficult to resist and I am not lonely for a wife who is busy starting a career five hundred miles away."

"Why you . . . you! You're not judging me, oh, no, but you accept every single word Jill told you as gospel truth! No wonder you think I'm available for your pleasure just whenever you get bored and want to . . . to while away a few minutes! You . . . ! Well, let me tell you . . ."

"Hannah," he interrupted, but she was too wound up, too hurt and angry and embarrassed to stop now.

"And anyway, why would anyone in their right mind look at . . . at me, when they could have Jill? Didn't she tell you I was fat? Hannah-ball, the bouncing ball! Does that sound like a . . . a femme fatale?" Her voice had risen and her eyes were glittering so that she could not see clearly. Perhaps that's why she had no time to escape those brutal hands when they clamped down on her upper arms and began to shake her.

"Hannah! *Dios*, stop it!" His voice was a growling command and she collapsed against his strength when the arms came around her. His hands stroked her head, playing havoc with her hairstyle, not that she even was aware of it. Her mind was taken up with the idea of what he must have thought of her . . . and her head flung up to stare at him.

"Lucian! What do you mean, am I not living with Bill? You mean you think I . . . that we . . . ?"

"And it is not true?" One of his hands rose to her face to brush away the hair that had caught against her wet cheeks.

"Of course it's not true! I mean—well, it is in a way, but not the way you mean," she finished inadequately.

She became aware of his hard body beneath her cheek as he heaved a sigh and she stepped away from him. He let her go.

"Your stepsister has a rather playful sense of humor, no? I'm afraid in many ways she is no more mature than Alice."

"But you're going to marry her," something prompted Hannah to say.

Immediately that cloak of hauteur dropped down over the man standing before her and she wished the floor would open up beneath her. It was none of her business.

"That does not concern you," Lucian told her in his rather more pedantic English. His cool survey of her person stung her into further indiscretion.

"It does if you're to be my brother-in-law. That would make me aunt to Kip and Alice, wouldn't it?"

The sun came out through the cold, blue clouds in his eyes as he answered her. "My apologies once more, *pequeña*. Perhaps I should leave you now before we endanger our future relationship." Before she knew what he was about, he had leaned over and taken her lips in a brief but intense kiss. "*Buenas noches, mi tizón*"—and he was gone before

she could question him again about calling
her names.

Several minutes later, when she heard the
front door slam and the sound of the jeep
starting up, Hannah moved and forced herself
to begin preparing for bed. Her appetite was
gone and she knew she would not be able to
concentrate on the theories of Augustus Le
Plongeon. Her glance slid off the thick volume
on her bedside table and focused somewhere
in the middle distance.

Without making a conscious effort to direct
her train of thought, she allowed certain ideas
to drift to the surface: Lucian still thought she
had taken advantage of Jill's being in New
York to steal her husband—as if such a thing
were even remotely possible! She supposed
she should be flattered, but there was a strong
reluctance to have him think so badly of her.

And then there was his surprising offer of
employment. Should she even consider it?
Could she? It was bad enough now, seeing
him leave with Jill to go out dancing, to meet
with their friends for dinner—and to disappear night after night up that staircase on the
opposite side of the *sala*. What would it be like
when they were married?

No. It was simply out of the question. Her
own feelings for Lucian did not bear close
examination, but she was afraid she was
becoming dangerously infatuated. Oh Lord!
Was that what it was?—the jolt of electricity
that could rob her of any will of her own, that

made her tremble at even the thought of his touch? Addiction was more like it—she was addicted to the man, and the only way to cure herself was to get out.

Her decision made, she waited impatiently to tell him. The morning after she had lain awake, desire wrestling with common sense, she arose early and wandered out to the balcony in time to see Lucian striding back from the stables. This had been a barebacked morning, when he had ridden the powerful stallion out into the surf, and his jeans clung darkly to his muscled thighs, riding low on his hips below the magnificent expanse of his bronzed chest. The sun caught the glint of the small medallion he wore nestled in the dark body hair and Hannah remembered the feel of it in her hand that day at Playa Santa Helena. He waved and she stepped back, conscious for the first time of her state of dishabille, the wrinkled gown and tumbled hair bearing mute testimony to her restless night.

By the time she had delayed going downstairs as long as she could, he had already gone and she was not sure whether she was relieved or disappointed. The children took up her day and it was only after they were settled in the kitchen with Carlotta for their supper that she escaped to the garden that ran between the *casa* and the stables. She desperately needed time to think. Last night's decision nagged at her and she searched in spite of herself for some rationalization for remaining where she could at least see him.

Masochist! she jeered at herself. You're like
some penniless child with her nose pressed
against the candy store window. Why don't
you face facts and get out while you still have
some chance of recovery?

She tugged restlessly at a flower head and
released its pungency into the softness of the
evening. What she needed was someone in
authority to say, All right, Hannah, there's
nothing for you here. Go pack your bags and
take the first thing out of here and then, for
being a good little girl, you may think of
Lucian on alternate Tuesdays until you work
him out of your system.

"Isn't it about time you were making
tracks?"

The words, spoken in Jill's driest accents
from immediately behind her, were so close to
what she had been thinking that Hannah
whirled around and almost lost her balance.
"Jill! You startled me!"

"Should I have knocked on the trellis before
breaking into your daydreams? Look, Hannah, just what happened last night? I left
here with the Keiths and I thought Lucian
was following with the Maitlands. None of
them showed up. Ted finally had to bring me
home." She didn't look entirely displeased at
the memory, but then her gaze sharpened on
Hannah. "What went on with you two?"

"What do you think? He took me to bed and
then begged me to make an honest man of
him."

"I'm not joking! You're getting entirely too

transparent with this crush of yours, Hannah, and no man is immune to open adulation!"

"Lucian is," Hannah retorted with more than a trace of bitterness. "He told me the first time I met him that he was immune to my type and you made good and sure he knew exactly what my type was, didn't you?"

She had the small satisfaction of seeing a look of embarrassment flicker across Jill's face, but it was quickly gone, replaced by the aloof perfection that had made her a name model in record time. "All's fair in love and war, and you were warned in the very beginning. Remember I told you Lucian was definitely not one of the fringe benefits? Well, it's time for you to leave, Hannah. If you don't have the fare, I can get it for you, but do yourself a favor, catch the next plane out of here, will you?"

Hannah was perfectly still, while all around her the darkening atmosphere filled with the sound of insects, the scents of sunbaked weeds, of moon-pale flowers, and a trace of the pungent sweetness of the stables. "Lucian has asked me to stay on and look after the children," she said quietly.

"I wouldn't advise it."

"You mean you're going to take them over?"

There was no time for an answer, for Lucian emerged from the whitewashed stables, let himself out of the feed-lot gate, and joined them. "I think my little Mixta will soon be looking with favor on the bold Conquistadore. Perhaps by this time next year, we may see the first of a new strain of horses on the island. And now, how about a swim before dinner?" His question seemed to fall impartially on them both, but before Hannah could voice a refusal, he continued. "Hannah, I believe the children are finished with their supper. Perhaps you will be so good as to stay with them tonight while Jill and I dine with the Maitlands. Carlotta and Manuel will be visiting their daughter in San Miguel."

Chapter Five

The fact that Lucian seemed to take her decision to stay for granted stung, but not as much as her speedy relegation to the rank of paid employee. While her position was not really that much different today from what it had been yesterday, she felt suddenly beyond the pale. Not that he had included her in all his plans before—not even Jill was privileged to accompany him everywhere he went, as if he were determined to retain a certain independence. It was going to be more uncomfortable than she had thought. No more polite pretense of guest status in the *casa*.

On the verge of reconsidering, matters were taken out of her hands. Kip, climbing on the coral boulders on the beach, tumbled and cut his leg rather badly and Hannah was suddenly indispensable. Dr. Alvarez pronounced him out of danger after several stitches and a course of antibiotics, plus tetanus vaccine, but warned that he must be kept quiet for at least a week to give the cut time to heal. Active little boys did not make the best of patients and she would have her work cut out for her, he declared.

That proved to be the case. Before the week was half over, she had exhausted her resources and Alice had tired of playing nurse to her little brother. While the little girl accompanied Jill and Lucian on several trips to other parts of the island, Kip and Hannah worked on the coconut-husk dolls, covered cigar boxes with shells and glued seeds onto cheap plates to make crude pictures.

On the evenings when Jill and Lucian dined in, Hannah joined them. She had eaten with the children the first two nights, in Kip's room, but Lucian put an end to that.

"You are not to spend every waking moment catering to the whims of those two, Hannah. You will leave them to Carlotta and join us in the courtyard, *por favor*."

She argued that she was hired to spend her time with the children but there was no contest; her arguments were met and conquered by Lucian's terse orders and she put on the yellow linen and joined them after settling the children.

The conversation was strained at first, for Jill didn't bother to hide her resentment at the intrusion. She talked exclusively to Lucian, gossiping about mutual acquaintances, ignoring his lack of response, and then began to tease him about returning to London to begin a new play.

"They'll forget all about you, darling, if you don't keep on reminding them. No point in living from revival to revival when you can give the public a new thrill every year."

"You're impossible to convince, are you not, *carina*? Have I not told you that I am finished with that sort of thing? It was a jest, a fluke, this knack I seem to have developed for appealing to the popular taste, but it is not work a man can take seriously."

"But Lucian! Don't tease me that way," Jill implored.

"Tell me why I should spend my time catering to the whims of a handful of bored urbanites whose attention span is limited to a few hours at best? *Dios!* Give me credit for more maturity than that, please! I prefer something I can sink my teeth into." He smiled that devastating smile that revealed nothing of his true feelings and Jill was left wondering whether or not he was serious.

Throughout all this Hannah remained a silent observer. Jill, when it finally dawned on her that Lucian meant every word he was saying, grew narrow-eyed and thin-lipped as she refilled her wineglass more often than usual.

Hannah reached the coffee and liqueur stage without having said more than a dozen words. When Lucian announced that he was going to a meeting of the museum board and invited them both to accompany him, Jill flounced off with a remark about inconsiderate hosts and Hannah, fighting against her every inclination, replied coolly that she planned to spend the evening writing letters.

Nor did Jill's temper improve during the next few days when Lucian seemed to spend most of his waking hours at some unspecified project that took him to the other side of the island. "Probably climbing those stupid rock heaps of his," she fumed, leafing through the newest fashion magazine in a way that threatened the pages. "If he thinks I'm going to stay home like a good little Mexican *hausfrau* he's got another think coming!"

Hannah, busy letting the hem out of one of Alice's dresses, hid her amusement by biting off a thread. A week ago she might have teased her stepsister over the linguistic absurdity, but she knew what it felt like to be the target of Jill's dissatisfaction.

Flinging down the magazine impatiently, Jill announced her plan to spend the afternoon with the Keiths aboard the schooner they were to sail on later during the week. Hannah was just folding the dress when the library door opened and Carlotta called her to the phone.

"Who is it?" she asked, hurrying across the *sala*. She had no idea of who could be calling her—except Lucian.

Carlotta shrugged and smiled teasingly on her way to the kitchen.

"Hello?"

"Hannah? Thank heaven! I had the devil's own time getting hold of you. It's me, Bill."

"Bill! Bill Tolland? What's wrong? Is it Rosa?" Her immediate concern was for his mother, who was diabetic and did not always take the best care of herself.

"No, Mama's fine. Look, Hannah, I need to talk to you. Can you get away and meet me somewhere?"

"Bill, are you crazy? Look, this must be costing you a fortune. Can't you write me?"

"You nitwit, I'm here—here in Cozumel!" he explained impatiently. "I'm at the airport, Hannah—now how do I get to your place? No, first I need to talk to you."

"Well, you're talking to me," she replied practically, "but Bill, what are you doing here? Look, can you hire a car? I can give you instructions on how . . ."

"Can't you meet me, Hannah? I want to talk to you in private before I meet Jill. She is there, isn't she?" His voice sharpened and Hannah began to have an inkling of why Bill had dropped everything to fly out to the island.

They arranged for her to pick him up in half an hour. She knew the way to the airport, although she wouldn't trust herself far off the beaten track. The other jeep was in the stables, and after explaining to Carlotta that she was meeting a friend, she let herself out the back door, to the accompaniment of the housekeeper's teasing remarks about an *enamorado*.

The second jeep was an older model, the same blue and candy stripe as the newer one, and was used primarily by Manuel, but he assured her that he would not be needing it until later on in the afternoon. Hannah climbed up behind the wheel and took a minute to study the dials and levers. She had driven mostly automatic transmissions, but this didn't look all that different from Rosa's Datsun and she had managed that once or twice.

She made it to within a mile of the airport. It was when she stopped at an intersection that she had trouble. With her foot on the clutch, she rolled out into the crossing still struggling to get the stick into first and there was no way she could have avoided being struck by the ancient truck that came rolling to an incomplete halt. She flinched, her hands over her ears, and when the noise of the collision died away, she peered apprehensively out the door to see a gathering of Mexicans, all chattering rapidly in Spanish and gesticulating wildly. The truck driver hopped out of his ramshackle vehicle and began shoving tumbled crates of chickens back into place and Hannah caught casual *de nada*s and a dismissing *"n'importa."*

The first thing she had thought of after the horrible noise died away was Lucian's face when he thought she had broken his Ix Chell; the second was Bill, waiting for her at the airport and wondering what had happened to her. With the help of a friendly bilingual

waiter on his way to work at a nearby hotel, it
was determined that neither vehicle was hurt,
nor were the drivers injured. They all seemed
to take a cavalier attitude about the whole
affair, and after one of the men tugged the
bent fender away so that it wouldn't scrape
the tire, Hannah decided not to mention the
various aches and pains that were making
themselves known.

She was almost too shaky to drive but there
was no help for it. She certainly couldn't stay
here in the middle of the street blocking
traffic, for sooner or later someone was bound
to come by who would recognize the jeep as
belonging to Casa Azul. She wanted to be well
away from here before that happened. Perhaps she could get the damage repaired before Lucian saw it. She could do without his
derision again, especially considering that
this time she was at fault.

Bill was pacing outside the small airport,
looking overheated and worried. Surprisingly
enough, she was little more than half an hour
late. Fortunately, the islanders did not seem to
take their accidents too seriously, although
she was beginning to feel more than a little
shaken by now. She switched off the engine,
pulled on the parking brake, and when Bill
strode over to assert that her vacation didn't
seem to have done her much good, she burst
into tears of pure nervousness.

"Good heavens, Hannah, you're all strung
up! What's happened to you? I thought you'd
be all browned and relaxed and ready to—"

He pulled her head against his chest and she dampened his shirt before she got herself in hand enough to explain.

"No, I'm not hurt," she protested, "just . . . you know! And besides, my stomach is beginning to feel queasy. Oh, Bill, could you please call the *casa* and have Manuel. . . . Oh, no, he can't," she wailed. "I have the jeep."

"Look, sit down before you fall down," Bill urged, taking her by the elbow to help her back up into the jeep. The canopy helped, for the sun was blazing down and she had come out with no hat, no sunglasses, and no lunch. She was seeing tiny black spots before her eyes and she told herself to breathe deeply and get herself in hand. It helped. She realized that Bill had been speaking and she hadn't heard a word he had said.

". . . so you see, I've got to try it, Hannah. It's my last chance and I can't throw it away. Will you help me?"

"Help you do what? I'm sorry, Bill, I wasn't paying attention."

"Oh, gee, honey, maybe we'd better get you to a doctor. I just said I need your help to make Jill notice me—to make her jealous, that's all. It's the only thing I can think of and I'd do anything to get her back again. You know how I feel about her. I never stopped loving her, but she had to get this modeling thing out of her system. Maybe now—oh, I'm a brute! Here you've conked your noggin and all I can talk about is my own troubles. Look, just promise me you'll go along with whatever I do, all right? We'd better . . ."

There was no time for more. From somewhere outside Hannah's limited field of vision, a dreadfully familiar voice demanded to know what was going on here.

Hannah practically fell out of the jeep and into his arms in her relief. "Oh, Lucian, I'm so sorry . . . I was going to have it fixed before you found out about it, but my head . . ."

"Stop babbling and tell me just what happened. Carlotta said you had a call from a friend at the airport and then someone saw my jeep involved in an accident." He steadied Hannah in the seat, not removing his arm from her shoulder as he glared at Bill, and even as Hannah mumbled an introduction, she was aware of the hardening chill that replaced Lucian's look of concern.

She was horribly afraid she was going to disgrace herself by being sick to her stomach and she plucked ineffectually at Lucian's arm and muttered something about lying down.

It was growing dark when she awakened in her own room. At first she thought she was all alone and all she could think of was, thank goodness she had gotten over the nausea. It had been replaced by a granddaddy of a headache, but anything was better than that awful greenish feeling.

"You're awake then? Finally!" It was Lucian and he looked anything but sympathetic.

Hannah flinched as his words jarred her throbbing head.

"Did I tell you I'm sorry?" she managed with a weak excuse for a smile.

Lucian stopped pacing to stride to her bedside and glare down at her. She was more than ever aware of the sharply defined cheekbones, the aquiline thrust of his nose, possibly because they were rimmed in white, as though he were controlling his anger with the greatest difficulty.

She wriggled down deeper in the bed, clutching the sheet protectively. Her mouth opened to apologize again and to offer to pay for the damages when he cut her off with what could only be a burst of profanity.

"Why did you do it? I believed you had settled down so well here, that you were on your way to forgetting, but no, at the first opportunity you . . ." He broke off and turned away and she breathed again. For a minute he looked as if he wanted to throttle her!

"I—I can only say again that I'm sorry, Lucian—Mr. Trent. I thought I could remember . . . I have driven a gearshift before but not very often and . . ." Her voice wobbled and she finished in a rush. "I'll pay you back. You can take it out of my salary."

This time she had gone too far. Lucian turned on her and his hands grabbed her shoulders through the thin stuff of the sheet as his eyes blazed down into her own. "Stop trying to avoid the issue! I don't care about the jeep! Wreck a dozen of them . . . break your silly little neck while you're at it!" He shook her and her head felt as if it were about to fall off.

Perhaps it was the bewildered pain that shimmered in her wide, brimming eyes— perhaps he merely regained control of his temper. The hands eased but did not release her, and when he sighed Hannah could feel the warmth of his breath playing across her damp face. "Hannah, Hannah, why did you do it? Did you write to him and ask him to join you here now that you were planning to remain? Could you not stand to be separated from your lover in spite of the pain his coming would inflict on your sister? Oh, Hannah . . . you drive me crazy with no effort at all. I look at you and forget what you are, forget what you've done." He shook her again and for one single moment she thought he was going to lean down and kiss her; he had that look in his eye.

"You look so young, so innocent, and I was so certain you were making a new beginning here," he finished, his words sounding like a plea.

Hannah tried to speak but no sound came. Her headache was forgotten in the pain he had inflicted on her heart and then, bubbling up from the very depths of her, came an anger that reached the surface and exploded. "You listen here, Lucian Trent, because I'm not going to tell you this again! What you believe about me just is not so, no matter what you think! You—I don't care if you . . ." That treacherous break in her voice again; she braced herself to get the words out before the tears came. "Go to . . . I don't *care* what you think! I've had a dozen lovers, a hundred of them! I'm only here for—for laughs, you know. I thought it might be fun to flaunt Bill in front of his ex-wife. I'm the wicked stepsister, didn't you know?" She began to laugh and his face got all blurred and then he gathered her up and was holding her against him, sitting on the edge of her bed.

"Hannah, Hannah . . . headstrong and headlong. Come, *mi tizón,* do not weep so. You are not the bad girl you pretend to be— there now, wipe your eyes." He pressed his handkerchief into her hand and she hiccupped and blotted her eyes. Things were getting hopelessly confused in her mind.

"Perhaps you were simply too young, *niña,* and when you were left alone it is only natural that you should cling to an older man, someone who represented security and strength to you."

An older man! She fought against a desire to laugh again. Oh, yes, there was heaven to be found in the arms of an older man, all right, but not Bill Tolland—it had never been Bill Tolland!

Lucian's voice continued to murmur soothingly. "It's all right, Hannah, my little bird. We will bring your friend here to the *casa* to stay. Jill will understand and perhaps things will sort themselves out when the two of you see each other again. What you did was not really wicked, *chiquita,* and no one blames you for it."

"H-how can you want me here—with your children, I mean—when you think I . . . you believe . . ."

"Hush, hush! The children adore you. I have seen nothing in your character to make me think you undesirable." His voice took on a deeper note of amusement. "In fact, I find you highly desirable, as you well know." His lips brushed against her hairline, the pressure forcing her face up to where she could see the expression in his eyes. Their deep blue light seemed to wash over her like a Caribbean wave and she clutched his crisp *guayabera* with both hands.

"Better now? Yes, I think we will have your Mr. Tolland share our hospitality. You will feel more secure with someone you know and love close by, no?"

"And Jill?" she probed tentatively, mystified by something she saw in his eyes. It was as though he were reading answers to questions that had not yet been posed, finding solutions to problems still unformulated.

"Leave Jill to me."

Of course. A familiar weight settled over her in the region of her heart as he laid her back down on her pillow and stood up. "Leave your sister to me, *amorcita,*" he repeated softly.

She was not ill, she kept insisting, nevertheless, Carlotta, fussing over her like a broody bantam, saw that she remained in bed until the following afternoon. The children were allowed in to see her briefly, with Kip limping up proudly to show off his stitches.

Jill came, concerned and sympathetic until she found Hannah in no danger of immediate expiration. Then her concern gave way to irritation. "Why couldn't you just leave without all these silly complications? If you thought you were sparing me the bother of the children, you couldn't be more wrong! We've had Alice every dratted minute since Kip got hurt and now I suppose we'll be stuck with him, too!"

Hannah shrugged. "Sorry, Jill," she offered helplessly. "Believe it or not, I didn't plan it. Anyway, I'm not really hurt, I just cracked my head on that pipe that holds up the canopy, that's all. A couple of aspirins and it'll be battle stations again."

"Lucian told me Bill had flown out," Jill charged. Her tone held suspicion and something else, something Hannah was too tired at the moment to decipher.

"He did. Do you care?"

"Care! Why on earth should I care? Bill's nothing to me! If he wants to waste his money chasing after you, more power to him. Maybe with a man of your own on the scene, you'll have sense enough to keep your greedy little paws off Lucian!"

There was no point in arguing. Besides, she had to lie quiet long enough to shed this headache, because she had no intention of

remaining in bed a minute longer than necessary. With Bill on the scene, all sorts of
complications could arise. Lucian's ideas
were impossible to understand and she had
all but given up trying to make him believe
there was nothing between her and Bill. The
only way she could prove her innocence
was ... A sudden wave of heat flooded her
face and throat, and with no pretense of good
manners, she turned her back and feigned
sleep.

Jill stood staring out the open balcony
doors, tapping her foot impatiently. The drift
of her cigarette smoke bothered Hannah but
not enough to protest. She was tired of trying
to second-guess everyone, tired of hidden
motivations, complex machinations. Her
open, straightforward nature writhed inward-
ly at something she sensed beneath the surface and she longed to recover and resume her
simple relationship with the children. So
much for sophistication! Maybe Jill was right
all along; she was nothing but a naive little
country girl.

Three days later Hannah was at the edge of
the pool watching while the children prac-
ticed the butterfly. They had had a demon-
stration the day before from Bill, who was a
surprisingly good swimmer, and they were
entranced by the showy stroke.

"I fink my wings are too little," Kip complained, thrashing madly in the shallow end.
Alice had remembered the body motion but

was having trouble coordinating foot and arm movements.

Bill and Lucian converged on them from opposite sides of the courtyard and Hannah reached hastily for her robe. She had grown accustomed to wearing a bikini now, but she was still not immune to Lucian's mocking scrutiny. He had been a model of rectitude since her official term of employment began, but there were occasional gleams in his eye that had nothing at all to do with her capabilities as a nanny.

"Have you had breakfast, Tolland? More coffee, perhaps?" Lucian offered, dropping into a chair at the round, glass-topped table. The low angle of the morning sun glinted off his thick, raven hair and Hannah fought back a sudden impulse to run her fingers through it.

The two men discussed the idea of driving to the site of some of the Mayan ruins on the other side of the island and Hannah listened in avidly as she blotted the children and put dry clothes on them. When they dashed into the kitchen to wheedle a second breakfast out of Carlotta, Lucian pulled a chair out for her and she sat down, helping herself to a cup of the thick, rich Mexican coffee.

"Would you care to accompany us, Hannah? I'm sure Carlotta would be glad to see to the children this afternoon."

Hannah would be overjoyed. She had stayed with the children every waking hour since her accident, more to avoid the company of the three adults than from any real sense of duty, but now she needed a break. "I'd love to go. I've wanted to see them ever since you showed me . . ." Her voice broke off as she caught the gleam of amusement in Lucian's eyes. He had showed her more than the sunrise and the ruins that day. She felt a guilty longing wash over her as she remembered in exquisite detail the feel of his hands and lips on her body.

Shortly after ten Jill emerged and plans were made to leave soon after lunch for the drive that would take perhaps two hours each way. Jill was not particularly enthusiastic but she made no demur.

"You wouldn't think that an island this size would have a two-hour drive on it, would you?" Bill asked, draining the coffeepot of its dregs. He looked fit and brown after only a few days on the island and so far, to Hannah's relief, there had been no indication that he planned to carry out his scheme to make Jill jealous.

The two men seemed to get along famously, to Hannah's surprise. Bill's manner to Jill was easy and slightly impersonal and to Hannah herself he was the same old affectionate, teasing ex-stepbrother-in-law. The children adored him, for there was a bit of Peter Pan in his makeup and they responded to it immediately.

Hannah was all ready to follow Bill, his camera case, and the ice chest of drinks into the back when Lucian intervened. It had been only a few days since her accident, he insisted, and she must take the front seat, where the roughness of the road would not have such an effect. Jill protested, but when Bill took her by the arm and led her around to the back and settled her on one of the cushions Manuel had provided, she didn't argue. Hannah was slightly embarrassed by the small incident, but once they turned off the pavement near Punta Morena, she counted her blessings.

There was more than enough to see, even conscious as she was of the large, strikingly virile man beside her, and Hannah was entranced by the moonscape beaches that were interspersed by small, sandy coves. Along most of the way there was simply too much vegetation to do more than catch glimpses of the sapphire Caribbean, but after bumping over miles of road fit only for the sturdiest of four-wheel vehicles, Lucian pulled off into a grassy clearing.

From the back came Jill's groans and Bill's teasing remarks about old bones—which had the effect of shutting her up immediately, to Hannah's amusement. She had noted more than once in the rearview mirror Jill's martyred expression and Bill's sardonic indulgence.

"This is quite small, but more intact than some of the other ruins, since it is protected from the sea as well as the jungle," Lucian informed them. He led them around the gray stone structure and Hannah listened with interest, although she was slightly disappointed. For some reason it was not quite what she expected—perhaps because it was within sight of the road and well cleared.

They climbed back into the jeep and proceeded, passing the only vehicle they saw during the whole trip, a truck carrying several men who had probably been working on one of the coconut or banana plantations in the area.

There were several more stops along the way for small, sometimes barely discernible heaps of stone and Jill remained in the car, looking more and more disagreeable. "Must we continue?" she demanded once when Bill took the time to shoot several views of one of the more intact ruins.

Hannah looked anxiously from Jill to Lucian. She didn't want the day to end, and not only because of the sight-seeing. For some reason, probably because of her recent shake-up, Lucian was being extraordinarily nice to her. She felt like a fraud, for there was nothing at all the matter with her, but all the same, she savored the feel of his hand on her arm as he helped her in and out of the jeep and his soft admonitions whenever she attempted to climb something he considered unsafe.

"I think perhaps Bill will be interested in the next one. We will go no further today, but you must not leave without seeing my favorite, bar one, perhaps—Aquada Grande."

They climbed back into the jeep and this

time Jill took the front seat and defied anyone
to dislodge her. Hannah was perfectly willing
to ride in the back. She felt better than she
had in ages, with a subliminal hum of excitement just under the surface of her consciousness bringing a becoming flush to her cheeks,
a sparkle to her honey-colored eyes.

They crept along, sometimes barely doing
five miles an hour, over terrain that changed
quickly from lush, junglelike growth to bar-
ren craters overgrown with crawling cactus to
light forest that was not unlike her own North
Carolina. When they finally stopped again
there was nothing at all to see except for the
trees and a sapling bar fence that cut across
the road.

Lucian pulled the jeep as far over as he
could and jumped out. Before he could come
around to the back, Hannah had eased herself
over the side and dropped to the ground. Bill,
laden with cameras and meters, assisted Jill,
who was voicing her opinion that there was
not a blessed thing to see and the heat was
sickening.

The weather was a bit oppressive. Ever
since that night a few weeks earlier when
Lucian had secured the boat against a storm
they had been threatened by bad weather that
never materialized. It was as if the forces of
nature were rehearsing for something spectacular, and as Hannah climbed the steep
incline Lucian indicated, she had to admit
that a thunderstorm would be welcome at this
moment. She couldn't make a move without

breaking out in perspiration in the uncomfortable humidity.

She came upon it suddenly. The others, Lucian on purpose and Jill because of a natural disinclination to exert herself, had let her lead the way, and when Hannah caught sight of the rough, gray walls looming over her she couldn't suppress a cry of delight. It was as if something shafted through her, something that whispered, This is what you've been waiting for.

"Do you like it?" Lucian said quietly. He had come up behind her, unnoticed, for once. A herd of elephants could not have torn her attention from the magnificent ruin.

It was by far the largest they had seen and it crowned the pyramid of tumbled stones with a regal dignity that neither time nor the elements could diminish. The sea had reached up to pull at its foundations, reducing what must have once been a narrow-stepped pyramid typical of other Mayan constructions to rubble. In splendid isolation, it faced the east, its roof gone, its face absent, only the compartmented walls remaining proudly aloof on their lofty foundation.

"It's so very fine, so . . . so real somehow," she breathed, enthralled by the spell it seemed to cast. "It looks out so patiently, as if it were waiting for someone—or something. Quetzalcoatl?" She looked up at Lucian who stood tall and bronzed, as if he belonged to the past and the present all at once. At that moment, she felt an interloper, for she could see that it meant something quite special to him.

"My shoes aren't made for this sort of thing," Jill groused from behind them. Bill had already swung out to one side and was crouched now for a low-angled shot of the profile with the three of them standing beside it.

"Now, Hannah," he called out, "how about getting out on the end of that thing—no, the other one. I want to get a shot of the sea washing up toward it and I need you there for scale as well as interest." He directed her out to what might have been a remnant of a terrace hundreds of years ago.

"Who's the model here anyway? If I'd known you were going to be doing this sort of thing I'd have worn something different," Jill said. "Move out of the way, Hannah, I'll do it."

"No, dollface, not this time. Your shoes, remember? Anyway, Hannah's a natural. I might even do a portfolio on her when we get home—how about it, Hannah?"

Hannah was in no position to comment one way or another as she edged out onto the shaky projection.

"Get down!" Lucian ordered suddenly, appearing from around the other side. "*Por Dios*, Tolland, are you crazy? The girl will break her neck!"

"Oh, no, not Hannah," Bill dismissed, flicking the cover on his light meter. "Hannah could climb the Eiffel Tower from the outside.

She'll tackle anything, won't you, love? There now, to the left just a bit—that's right, hold it!"

"Hurry up," she cried waveringly. Down was an awfully long way from her precarious perch and after one sickening glance Hannah kept her eyes trained on the horizon. At least it was cool out here, for the movement of air from the open sea evaporated the fine film of perspiration that beaded her body, whether from the weather or her nerves she wasn't sure.

"All right, now, get yourself back here. Slowly!" Lucian barked. He had come halfway out onto the heap of loose rocks to meet her and as he held out a hand she began to edge toward it. Three tentative steps and their fingers touched, and with a sigh of relief she practically fell on top of him.

"Wow! Never again! What is it, acrophobia? The fear of heights? For the next few days, I don't even want to reach for a book on the top shelf!" She made no attempt to dislodge herself from Lucian's arms as he held her close for a minute before climbing back down to where the others waited.

Bill snapped his lens cover on and hurried up to take her arm once they were safely down. "Thanks a million, sweetheart. You're a natural. We'll make a cover girl of you yet!" He took her hand as if it were a matter of course and led her away from Lucian, leaving both Jill and Lucian glaring after them.

And so it goes, Hannah thought wryly. She

had all but forgotten Bill's proposed scheme and now it seemed she had no choice but to go along with it. Anyway, she had no desire to become a model and if this was all he intended—to make Jill look to her professional laurels—Hannah wouldn't mind obliging. Certainly Lucian could have no complaint about that, for he was only concerned that Hannah had broken Jill's marriage up, not her career.

They spent another half hour at the ruin, and it was only as Bill reluctantly put away his camera to accompany Jill back to the jeep that Hannah had a minute to herself to sit alone inside one of the small rooms and simply absorb the atmosphere. Lucian was somewhere about; she didn't know just where and for the moment she didn't care. The ambience of the place was almost overwhelming and she wanted to let it wash over her, leaving behind a deeper understanding of the proud people who had built the temple hundreds of years ago.

As if sensing her need to be alone, Lucian stayed away. He finally came into her field of vision when he followed the tumbled heap of stones at the water's edge, and reluctantly she stood up, brushing the seat of her jeans, and hopped nimbly down to where he waited. When he extended a hand, she took it with no second thought—such was their rapport at the moment.

"Had enough?" he asked softly.

"I could never have enough," she replied in

the same tone. "It's almost as if you could reach a hand out and see it disappear through time to clasp the hand of someone who lived hundreds of years ago. Do you think that's silly?" She looked up at him anxiously.

"No, *querida*, not at all." His fingers entwined with hers and he turned to gaze up the slope to the haunting ruin on top. "Perhaps we'd better be leaving, though. It's a long way back and there is still one thing I wish to show you."

"Not another ruin?"

"No, Hannah, not today. Perhaps another day I will show you Tumbra del Caracol, but after this anything would be an anticlimax."

Jill was in the front seat again, but Hannah's feeling of well-being persisted as Lucian handed her into the back to Bill's hands. She settled down onto the cushion, feeling a warm glow of happiness and whenever she caught Lucian's clear eyes on her in the rearview mirror, she smiled at him unselfconsciously. Nothing could spoil the new understanding they seemed to have reached today.

They stopped in a cleared coconut plantation to eat sandwiches and drink *cervesa*, the Mexican beer, and Jill slathered on another layer of sunscreen and frowned at a broken nail. Hannah's browned face and arms sustained mosquito bites and the sweltering heat with no signs of permanent damage and she drank two of the cool beers before Lucian laughingly put an end to it.

"We can't have you falling out of the jeep, *niña*, for I know you are unaccustomed to too much alcohol, especially in this heat."

Jill seemed peeved at the indulgent teasing note in his voice but Hannah simply flopped onto her back with a beatific smile and closed her eyes. "Wake me when you're ready to move on. I think I could stay here a week!"

"You've turned into a sponge, darling," Bill commented, tickling her upper arm with a twig. Jill frowned even more, Hannah saw through lazily slitted lashes.

They finally reached the pavement again, but instead of turning back on the new airport road, as they had come, they continued to go south, turning off after a short while onto a graded coral track. Hannah saw several of the ferocious-looking iguanas sunning themselves on rocks along the drive before they pulled up under a grove of palms close to a construction site. Once more Lucian climbed out and held his arms up to Hannah in the back and this time she slid almost bonelessly into them. She felt bemused with sun and *cervesa* and a wonderful sense of well-being.

"I think I'll sit this one out, if it's all the same to you, Lucian," Jill said. Bill climbed into the driver's seat beside her and then seemed to think better of it and got out to join Hannah and Lucian.

The three of them surveyed the building under construction on its high vantage point overlooking the sea. It was not unlike the Casa Azul, although the courtyard in the center was only a dusty clearing littered with building materials and heavy equipment so far.

Bill moved closer to Hannah and draped a casual arm across her shoulders and she cut her eyes to where Lucian stood. "So far we don't seem to have made much of an impression," he said grimacing.

"On a personal or a professional basis?" she asked.

"On any basis that will get a rise out of her. She just lolls there looking more beautiful than any other woman would after a day at the beauty parlor. The new hairstyle is great, isn't it?" His eyes had that spaniel look again and Hannah squeezed his hand sympathetically. She knew the feeling, unfortunately.

"If you're ready to go," Lucian suggested curtly, "we'll be off." His easy mood seemed to have dissolved on the steamy air.

"What's it going to be, Lucian?" Hannah ventured, following his stiff back to the jeep.

"No importa."

She clambered up into the back of the jeep with no help and watched as Jill leaned her head against Lucian's shoulder, wondering in a little-girl voice if they were headed home at long last. "Give me civilization and all its trimmings," she murmured.

For the next few days Bill hounded her steps whenever she had a minute free from the children until Hannah finally confronted him in the garden after dinner one night.

"Look, Bill, I'm willing to go along with anything within reason, but this is ridiculous! Even with Jill, you never hung around wasting time this way. You always had something to do, somewhere to go. Take pictures! Go sight-seeing! I can't take any more of Lucian's ferocious stares."

"Trent! What does he have to do with it? I should think he'd be happy that I'm not hanging around Jill. I mean, after all, they're supposed to be in love, aren't they?"

Involuntarily, Hannah's shoulders drooped. "He's of the old school. Age of chivalry and all that. He told me having you here would hurt Jill's feelings because he thinks I'm the one who broke up your marriage in the first place."

"What? That's ridiculous!"

"Thanks," she replied sarcastically.

Bill pulled her to him in an easy embrace. "Oh, you know what I mean, honey. You're pretty super yourself, but I happen to be a one-woman man." He propped his forehead against her own and attempted a grin. "For all the good it does me. Seems there's no market for old faithful types like me."

Hannah was not even aware that they weren't alone until Lucian spoke from behind them. "Hannah, if you can find the time, the children could use your services." He glowered at her as if he had caught her in some indiscretion and she heaved a sigh and moved away from Bill. Was no one happy anymore? Poor Bill moped around as if he'd lost his last friend, Lucian was out of sorts with them all, and Jill seemed to be avoiding everybody. As for Hannah herself, only during the day, when all her thoughts were taken up with keeping up with two superactive children, could she forget the ache that was becoming a permanent feature in the region of her heart. She had been a fool to stay and even more of a fool to have agreed to Bill's plans, for, no matter what she did, Lucian glared at her disapprovingly.

Matters seemed to come to a head one evening when the four of them were lounging in the courtyard after dinner listening to music. Jill's feet were keeping time and she was eyeing Lucian as if willing him to dance with her. Bill, knowing full well that his ex-wife would rather dance than eat, stood up and held out his hand to Hannah.

"Come on, honey, let's not let it go to waste. After all, tropic nights and pretty women don't grow on trees."

Reluctantly, Hannah let him pull her to her feet. He had only two days left and the poor dear looked desperate enough to do something foolish. She drifted around the softly lighted courtyard held closely in his arms wishing she knew how to comfort him. There simply wasn't a chance that Jill would realize she had made a mistake and go back to him. Given a choice between Bill and Lucian, what woman would take Bill Tolland, as nice as he was?

Lucian and Jill joined them and as the two

couples circled on the smooth tile floor under a quarter moon, Hannah decided to make one last all-out effort. She moved her arms up around Bill's neck and insinuated herself as close to him as she could. She felt nothing; he might as well have been Carlotta for all the emotion he aroused in her.

She caught sight of Lucian and Jill and a wrenching pain shot through her. Lucian was leaning down to catch something Jill was saying and, even as he caught Hannah's look, he placed a light kiss on her silver blond hair.

The Latin beat ended and a slow, dreamy love song wafted out into the flickering light of the courtyard. Hannah was supremely conscious of the man across the shimmering pool from her, and when Bill grew more openly affectionate a mood of recklessness seized her and she responded by placing a kiss on his chin. When his steps stopped altogether and he kissed her on the mouth, she stood frozen in misery. Poor, dear Bill—poor Hannah, too—both of them in love with someone else and unable to do anything about it.

The record stopped with a grinding screech and the lid of the stereo was slammed down furiously. Guiltily, Bill and Hannah broke apart to see no sign of the other couple.

"Looks as if you got a reaction, at least," she whispered ruefully.

"But from whom?" he shrugged, following her slowly into the *sala*.

They separated then, with a brief good night, and Bill crossed the room to climb the

stairs to the west wing. That in itself was the
final irony, Hannah thought, for until he
came Lucian and Jill had had the whole wing
to themselves. She wondered if his presence
made any difference to them. Probably not,
she thought, sighing, and continued on her
way to her own room.

Friday morning was off to a bad start before
Hannah even got out of bed. She had lain
awake long into the night, her eyes burning
and her throat aching thickly as she acknowl-
edged to herself that she was miserably,
irrevocably in love with Lucian. No wonder
she had gone along with Bill's poor scheme
last night; she was far more anxious to sting
Lucian with jealousy than to further any of
Bill's ambitions. Not that it had done any
good. Lucian had simply stalked into the *sala*
and turned off the music—prompted by some
misguided idea of Jill's suffering, no doubt.

Goodness, she thought, wriggling up in bed
to stare balefully out the balcony doors, why
can't everyone simply be open about their
emotions? Bill could tell Jill he still loves her
and get slapped down for his pains, Lucian
could marry Jill and put an end to any possible uncertainty she might be harboring, and
Hannah—where did that leave Hannah? The
butt of a few jokes from Lucian or the recipient of his careless attentions. He admitted he
found her desirable, even if he suspected her
morals weren't all they should be.

In the midst of this painful soul searching,

Jill walked in unannounced. "Well, you certainly made a cheap spectacle of yourself last night, didn't you?" she sniffed. "Lucian was thoroughly disgusted!"

"It's none of his business, is it? And you told me I could help myself to Bill as long as I didn't distract Lucian."

"Distract! As if you could!" Jill, already made up and beautifully dressed in a turquoise cotton gauze caftan, jammed a cigarette in her holder and lighted it to inhale deeply. "Well, if you want to pick over my leftovers, I don't see why I should care. He'll never love anyone else, though. Go ahead and marry him—he'll still be mine whenever I snap my fingers."

"But then, why should you snap your fingers? You'll be Mrs. Lucian Trent, won't you? I don't imagine even Lucian would allow you to keep a spare."

Jill turned away impatiently, her thin shoulders hunched as she tapped her teeth with a scarlet fingernail. "Lucian—when I first met him he was guest of honor at a theater party and every woman there would have given her right eye to warm his bed."

"Including you," Hannah pointed out, sliding out of bed and reaching for her hairbrush.

"You're darn right, including me, and one of these days I'm going to do it, too, and it won't be too long off!"

Round eyed, Hannah stared at her, the brush dangling loosely in her hand. "But I thought . . ."

Jill whirled around and glared at her. "I'm not that big a fool, Hannah-ball! Why buy the cow when the milk's free?"

"To put it crudely," Hannah murmured, aware of a strange feeling spreading throughout her body. So Jill had managed, for all her insinuations, to hold Lucian at bay. No wonder he had been so anxious for a little extracurricular activity when another woman came onto the scene—especially one he considered very experienced at that sort of thing! Lucian was an extremely virile man, one who had been married for a short while and who had certainly never lacked for willing cooperation from any number of beautiful women.

"It's this insufferable island," Jill continued, breaking in on Hannah's speculations. "Once I can get him weaned from this sort of thing, we can go back to London or maybe New York. There's no reason why the children shouldn't stay on here—after all, they didn't see all that much of Larice when she was alive, so why should they have to stick like a couple of ticks to Papa? No, we'll have old Goodge back—unless you'd care to stay on after we leave?" She turned to look questioningly at Hannah.

"Look, Jill, are you sure you're doing the right thing, trying to take Lucian away from here? Somehow I think he means it when he says he's given up all that. He'd never be happy running around with people like Ted and Sylvia. They're brass, he's gold."

"Boy, you've got it bad, haven't you, poor old

sister mine? Well, he's gold, all right. Wherever we decide to live, you can bet it will be in
style. Lucian's loaded even without what he
makes on his hit plays."

"Then you can't lose, can you?" Hannah
asked resignedly, suddenly tiring of the whole
conversation. "I'm going to shower now. See
you downstairs, I suppose."

Standing under the rushing lukewarm
water a few minutes later Hannah wished
wholeheartedly that she had never heard of
Cozumel. Maybe then she would have settled
for Bill and he for her—and in time he might
have forgotten Jill. If she had never met
Lucian Trent, Bill might have filled her every
need; he was personable, kind, witty, and
moderately successful in his chosen field. If
she didn't quiver at his touch, melt when he
kissed her, was that any great loss? From
her limited experience, she had concluded
that that sort of mindless urgency was best
avoided.

Chapter Six

Two days later, Lucian persuaded Bill to postpone his departure for a cruise to newly developed Cancun and Isla Mujeras, a tiny fishing island further north. Jill groaned at the prospect, but when Bill expressed eagerness she gave in with no more than token resistance.

When Lucian announced that Kip and Alice were to spend the weekend on the mainland with the Maitlands' grandchildren, Hannah's own excuse for declining was lost.

They got underway immediately after an early breakfast, with Jill complaining about the ungodly hour, but still managing to look as if she had stepped out of the pages of *Vogue*. Hannah had opted for cut-off jeans, taking her bikini and a shift in Carlotta's basket. The boat boasted a large comfortable stateroom, so there was plenty of room to change if she decided Cancun rated something more formal.

"Pure fantasy land" was Bill's comment as they cruised at a leisurely rate along the white, palm-dotted shores. Lucian slowed over an occasional reef to allow him to admire the coral growth that reached up almost to the surface in some places and they reached Cancun in time for a look around before lunch.

Hannah was not terribly impressed. She much preferred the sparse, scattered development on Cozumel, but by lunchtime she was not at all reluctant to relax in the air-conditioned comfort of one of the brand-new restaurants. Bill had fallen back to walk with her most of the time they had spent strolling around, and whenever he thought Jill might be looking he had nuzzled her or dropped a casual kiss on top of her head. She didn't mind Jill's derisive looks half so much as Lucian's glowering. Evidently he was still laboring under the idea of protecting Jill's tender sensibilities.

The thought stung her into further indiscretion and she lost no opportunities to lean against Bill's shoulder and murmur inane words in his ear. "Oh, darn, my feet are tired," she whispered seductively, aware of the other two just behind them.

"Just be thankful they're not the size of

mine," Bill whispered back tenderly, "then you'd really have something to ache!"

"Are you ready to go now?" Lucian growled from behind them. They had given in to Jill's demands to window-shop after lunch, for many of the shops would not open until later on in the afternoon.

"Oh, Lucian, must we?" Jill agonized. She had done more than hint that she had no interest in another underdeveloped fishing village and now Lucian looked at Bill, his thick black brows raised questioningly.

Bill shrugged. He might be holding hands with Hannah but it was obvious—to her, at least—that if Jill wanted to spend the day at a dentist's office, Bill would have been eager to accompany her. He took her by surprise, however. "Maybe you and Jill can stay here and wait for the shops to open and Hannah and I can wander around on our own. After all, unless I can persuade her to come home with me, we don't have much time left together." He hugged her to his side and looked soulfully at her from liquid brown eyes. "You can't imagine how lonely it is there at home without you, honey."

Hannah almost strangled! He might be lonely, all right, but not for Hannah. How could he imagine that Jill would be taken in by such melodramatic bilge!

Jill might not be taken in but she was definitely put out. No matter how many attentive lovers she had in tow, she couldn't stand for one of them to defect, it seemed, and Lucian—oh, no, Lucian was thunderous!

"We'll secure the boat, then, if we're to remain here for the day. Come along and fetch your belongings and I'll take a room for you to change in later on," Lucian ordered stiffly. He was obviously not pleased at the change of plans.

Bill was delegated to bring Jill's case back while she waited in an air-conditioned lobby and the three of them trekked off under a broiling sun to the jetty.

Hannah gathered up Jill's things and her own and handed Jill's case up to Bill. She had stepped up onto the beach, her own basket over her arm, when Lucian called her back.

"Here, hold a finger on this toggle switch, will you? There seems to be a short somewhere." He was just inside the bulkhead hanging over the portside engine cover and Hannah, her finger on the designated switch, gazed down on his broad shoulders. Through the open weave of his black knit shirt, she could see the gleaming bronze of his shoulders, and it was all she could do not to reach out a hand to him.

"See you back at the hotel," Bill called, strolling back the way they had come. The jetty was at one end of the large, blindingly white hotel and inside the cool dimness of the lobby waited Jill, looking impossibly lovely in a white silk pants suit splashed with orange poppies. Hannah frowned down at her own bare brown legs.

"How long must I hold it? My finger's getting cramped."

"Not much longer, *pequeña*," Lucian answered her, dropping the cover over the Gray Marine and standing up to wipe his hands off on a bit of waste. "A moment only," he promised, jumping ashore to do something with a line. He was back aboard almost before she had time to wonder and he edged her aside as he took the wheel, a strange smile on his thin features.

"We're moving! Lucian, we're drifting away!" Hannah exclaimed, leaning over the side and watching as the jetty grew smaller in the distance.

Half an hour later, Hannah still sat in the fighting chair aft, her back turned stubbornly away from the man at the controls. She had quickly overcome her initial burst of excitement when she discovered that Lucian was kidnapping her. His motive was obvious; she was to leave Bill alone and stop making Jill unhappy. The only thing she couldn't figure out was how a man who professed to love a woman could go off cheerfully and leave her to spend the day with another man—a man she had once cared enough for to have married.

"Still sulking?" he called provocatively over the low roar of the engines. They had slowed down to a few knots and there was hardly even a wake to disturb the glassy stillness of the ultramarine blue water.

"I'm not sulking," she replied indignantly. "I am simply waiting for you to get tired of this ridiculous game and take me back. Jill's not going to be very happy with either of us, you know."

The engines throbbed with a low, gutsy growl and Hannah could feel the vibrations all through her spine as she stared stubbornly at the smudge on the horizon that was Cancun.

"I thought you wanted to see Isla Mujeras. Or were you only pretending an interest? Believe me, *pequeña,* you would not be the first woman to employ such devious tactics to gain her own ends."

Indignantly, Hannah swiveled the chair around. "And what are my so-called ends supposed to be? I think you're astoundingly conceited as well as completely insensitive! Now, how about turning this thing around and taking me back to Cancun. Bill and I have a lot of packing to do if we're to leave tomorrow." That last was purely off the top of her head, but the minute the words were out she recognized the truth of them. She simply couldn't afford to hang around for Lucian to toy with while he made up his mind to set the date with Jill. Talk about having your cake and eating it too!

Without bothering to answer, Lucian cut the engines completely and moved forward with the ease of someone thoroughly at home on a boat. From where she sat glowering Hannah could see him ease the anchor into

the water and play out the line, making it fast
with a quick motion of the wrist. He returned
to drop back into the cockpit and two more
steps brought him to where she sat twisting
the chair nervously on its swivel base. Hands
on lean hips, he raked her thoroughly with
chilly eyes, making her miserably conscious
of her hot, messy appearance. There was not a
breath of air and she was still wearing the
cut-off jeans and yellow top she had started
out in early that morning.

"Shall we deal with your comments one at a
time, *pequeña*? Your ends, for instance, are
obvious. You are not in love with Bill Tolland
and yet you persist in using him to aggravate
your sister. It is quite clear that you are
jealous of her and you will lose no opportunity
to make . . ."

"Jealous! Of Jill? You're crazy!" she broke
in.

Those remote blue eyes became strangely
opaque as Lucian stared down his arrogant
nose at her and Hannah felt herself at a
distinct disadvantage, seated as she was beneath his tall, imposing figure. She jumped to
her feet, an action that brought her uncomfortably close to him, and with the chair
behind her knees there was no retreat.

"And you, *mi tizón,* you are asking for what
you are about to get." Even as he spoke his
hands came out to grasp her arms and she
twisted her face away, afraid of his punishing
kiss, afraid he would discover just how wrong
he was about her motives. Instead of pulling

her closer and forcing his kisses on her, however, Lucian twisted her so that she lay across his raised knee, and before she could recover herself he had administered two hard spanks to her bottom.

Outraged and humiliated, Hannah pulled herself away from him and dashed for the cabin. She made it safely and managed to slam the door and leaned back against it, panting, for several moments before she realized that he hadn't even bothered to follow her. Irrationally, she was made even angrier at the knowledge, and when the floodgates opened she felt behind her for a lock, found none, and slid down into a heap against the door.

After perhaps five minutes, she fumbled in her pockets for a tissue and blew her nose. Then, struggling to her feet, she made her way to the compact bathroom where she dashed cold water on her face. Back in the cabin again, she faced the embarrassing prospect of emerging from her sanctuary.

Darn the man, he'd probably be waiting for her, just standing there watching the door, ready to laugh at her red-rimmed eyes and her complete loss of dignity.

Well, let him laugh! At least he'd take her back now and she and Bill could cut their losses and get back to where they belonged. Nothing back home had ever reduced her to such a state of abject misery! Of course, nothing back home had ever even hinted at

the heights of trembling expectancy she had
glimpsed since meeting Lucian Trent either.

Enough of this maudlin introspection, she
chided herself. Back ramrod straight, she
opened the door and stepped boldly out into
the open cockpit. Her chin was tilted at an
uncomfortable angle and she braced herself
against Lucian's derision. Not only did it not
come, nothing came. Blinking, she looked
around her. There was no one there, no one at
all.

She glanced back down the short companionway to the other stateroom but the door
was hooked back and the room was obviously
empty. Uncertainly, she moved toward the
stern of the *Sunbird* and peered up across the
bow, but there was no tall, imposing figure
hauling up the anchor line—no Lucian anywhere!

"Ah, *pobre niña,* are you finished with your
tears for the moment? Tantrum all done?"

She spun about swiftly, catching her
breath, to see him floating, ankles crossed
and one arm at a relaxed angle above his
head. He had stripped down to brief black knit
trunks and the sight of that tanned, virile
body drifting lazily on the surface of the
aquamarine water was the last straw! She
was hot, sweaty, emotionally drained and
there he was, as cool and casually friendly as
if they had parted a week ago after tea instead
of only minutes ago after his outrageous,
unwarranted attack.

"What do you think you're doing?" she demanded illogically.

"We're in for a bit of a storm, *pequeña,* and before I take the helm once more to seek shelter, I wished to cool off and relax. I suggest you join me." He was insinuating that she could do with a bit of cooling off, no doubt, and she stiffened.

Before she could even open her mouth to tell him just what she thought of his suggestion, however, he continued ruefully, "But then your indomitable pride would never permit you to accept my invitation, would it? No, the very last thing you could allow yourself would be a sensible, refreshing dip before we raise anchor."

It was his tone of voice even more than his words, and without even pausing to consider, Hannah stepped up on the railing and dived over the side, going deep beneath the translucent surface, feeling the unexpected chill of the lower layers as well as the pull of the current. She surfaced some distance from where Lucian drifted indolently over the choppy surface and struck out toward the hazy blur she assumed was Cancun.

He let her go for perhaps a hundred feet before hailing her. "Come now, it is time to board the boat and prepare to outrun the storm. You have cooled off a bit, no?"

She trod water then, revolving slowly to study the sky and it was with a strange, empty feeling in her middle that she saw the horizon that had been such a lovely shade of cerulean hours before covered with a roiling, dark gray mass. Even as she watched in dreadful fascination, the seething mass, its top edges lined in pale gold, seemed to climb higher over her head. Kicking out instinctively, she raced for the security of the *Sunbird*, her stroke even less polished than usual in her haste.

Lucian was there before her, waiting patiently, and she allowed him to give her a boost on the awkward rope boarding ladder. By the time he followed her over the side her body was already covered with fine chill bumps, as much from her own apprehensions as from the rapidly cooling air.

"Go inside, Hannah, and dry yourself off. We are in no danger in spite of the ominous looks of the clouds." Lucian stepped up to the controls without even bothering to pick up the towel that was flung carelessly across the back of the fighting chair and Hannah hesitated.

"Isn't there anything I can do?"

"*Nada, gracias*. Go below, dry yourself, and put on some dry clothes. We will be anchoring again in a protected cove within a few minutes and then you shall see to something for us to eat. Coffee would be welcome, would it not?"

Doubtfully, she did as he asked. Her clothes were feeling clammy and she would be glad enough to shed them. If she'd only taken the time to change into her bikini, she'd have had these to change into again instead of the dress she had brought along for Cancun. It was all

Lucian's fault, of course. He had taunted her
into diving overboard in her clothes, but there
was nothing to be gained from confronting
him with her accusations now. He'd only
laugh and tease her about being headstrong
and headlong. Besides, the storm, even
though he seemed completely undisturbed by
it, took precedence over any differences between the two of them. Lucian might not be
worried, but to Hannah's inexperienced eye
the prospects were alarming.

She hurried off to the bathroom and showered, hair and all. If she had to wear unsuitable clothes, at least she'd be spared the
discomfort of a coating of salt on her skin. She
blotted herself on the thick towel provided and
pulled the shift over her head, wishing she
had thought to bring along a change of underwear. Later on her nylon bra and briefs would
be dry enough to wear but at the moment
they were far too wet and clinging to think
of putting on. All the same, as she considered her image in the small mirror, she felt
terribly vulnerable in the light cotton shift
with its flaring bias cut and narrow shoulder
straps.

Eyeing the built-in storage compartment,
she considered the possibility of finding a pair
of Lucian's jeans and a shirt of some sort.
After all, he still had the clothes he had shed
before swimming to put on if he got chilled.
Without a second thought, she opened the
locker door and rifled through the several
items that swayed on the hangers, finally

selecting a natural weave cotton outfit consisting of drawstring trousers and a pullover shirt with a kangaroo pocket and a hood. It would be miles too large, of course, but with the drawstring it could be made to fit.

She had changed within two minutes flat, rolling up the pant legs and sleeves to a workable length. It felt warm and soft, if far from fashionable, and she quickly suppressed the small tingle of excitement at the thought of Lucian's clothes against her naked body.

They were moving now, had been ever since she emerged from the shower, and there was a noticeable roll that had been absent before. One glance through the porthole revealed the reason—crisp whitecaps ran them a losing race as they chased the wind, and even as she peered anxiously at the sky, a flurry of raindrops spattered her face. She closed both the portholes in the larger stateroom and crossed the companionway to close the single one in the smaller room before making her way up the three steps to where Lucian stood at the controls. He could have remained inside, for the controls were duplicated there, but he preferred to be outside where the wind tore through his hair, flinging it forward over his brow, and whipped his jeans against his braced legs.

"Can I do anything?" she yelled over the sound of the two powerful engines.

"Coffee and sandwiches, perhaps?"

Nodding, she turned away and hurried to the small, well-designed galley. A place for everything and everything in its place, she remembered her mother saying, referring to the mess Hannah often left in her own room when she dashed out to play. Well, her mother would have heartily approved of the *Sunbird*, for the galley held everything anyone could need and each item was ingeniously stored away in such a manner that it couldn't be dislodged by any but the most extreme weather.

By the time she had put together two thick corned beef and mustard sandwiches and made two steaming mugs of coffee they were once more cruising at a moderate rate of speed and the water seemed to be considerably smoother.

"Ready now?" she asked, coming out to where Lucian was studying the coastline. "This isn't Cancun," she exclaimed, setting the tray down on the wide shelf that lay behind the windscreen.

"Of course not, *niña*. Nor is it Isla Mujeras. We are cruising along the coast of the mainland now. Somewhere in the vicinity is the cove I seek. Ahh, that looks good." He helped himself to one of the sandwiches and munched with seeming unconcern as he steered the boat with one capable hand.

Hannah's own sandwich lay untasted as she stood beside him, peering into the premature gloom at the inhospitable-looking shoreline. It seemed low and marshy, for the most part, and Hannah could see no sign of a sheltering cove. Then they swung around a low-lying point and there, between two stunted rocky cliffs, was an inlet of sorts into which Lucian swung the bow of the *Sunbird*. Feeling the deck vibrating beneath her feet from the harnessed power of the engines, Hannah watched apprehensively as the channel narrowed and twisted; it seemed to her that the scrubby trees would offer scant protection, but once past the offset opening the water was as calm as a mirror.

Lucian cut the engines and allowed the boat to drift almost to the other side of the cul-de-sac before lowering the anchor. Neither of them spoke a word while all this was going on, and not until the bow had swung around to face the direction of the wind did Lucian drop back down into the cockpit beside her.

"Your coffee is cold, *pequeña*. Is there more?"

Suddenly aware that she was no longer shivering, Hannah shook her head. "But that's all right. I can drink it lukewarm." She was hungry now that the tension of seeking shelter was over and she bit into her thick sandwich eagerly, looking up to see Lucian's eyes upon her. A smile warmed his face, a smile that looked almost indulgent.

It was the deceptive light, of course. It couldn't be all that late, but she could barely see across the cockpit to where he lounged easily against one of the canopy supports. Still without speaking, he reached out a hand and emptied her coffee over the side.

"Hey, wait a minute! What am I supposed to drink?" she protested.

"I can do better than that. Come below, *carina*, before the mosquitos discover your tender, delectable flesh."

Hannah followed him wordlessly down the three steps and turned to the galley on the starboard. Lucian extracted a bottle of wine from the tiny gas refrigerator and nodded to the cabinet behind her. "If you will be so kind as to hand me two glasses," he suggested, neatly uncorking the bottle, "we will continue our dinner down here. Is there enough meat for another sandwich?"

Helplessly, she turned and got out the remaining meat, the dark bread, and mustard. She had an idea this was all a big mistake, for there was an intimacy here in the close confines of the small compartment, especially with the weather growing more and more threatening outside. "The storm," she ventured. "Will it last very long?"

He shrugged. "A dry shift. There will be wind, perhaps a smattering of rain, but no lightning to frighten you, *amada*. It will be over within an hour." He bit into his sandwich with strong, white teeth, thanking her with a nod.

"Do you think the others are worried about us?"

"I doubt very much that they are thinking about us at all."

The wine was dry and fairly fruity, a rosé with an unfamiliar label. Hannah drank thirstily. Outside she could hear the wind whining through the tops of the low trees and she could visualize them bending low to its power, but she could see nothing. It was almost completely dark. For long minutes the silence ticked by, broken only by the soft, sucking sounds of water against the fiberglass hull.

"Do you think . . . could you turn on a light?" she ventured after a while.

"I'm afraid not. Does the darkness frighten you?"

"No, not really. It's just . . . well, I can't see to clear away the things here in the kitchen."

"The galley, my little land lover," he laughed. The low sound seemed to set up a reciprocal vibration along her spine.

Nervously she sat her glass down, sloshing some of the wine out over the side in her haste. "That's landlubber."

"I prefer the word *lover*—don't you?" There was no mistaking the low, insinuating note in his voice now.

"Why don't we go upstairs and wait for the storm to be over. It's breathless down here!"

He moved beside her in the gloom and she edged away, but there was nowhere to go in the cramped space. "Breathless. Yes, *amada*, that is the exact quality I felt here myself." She could hear the smile in his voice and panic covered her like a warm, wet blanket.

"Stop calling me that, Lucian! I'm not your *amada* and we both know it!"

"And whose *amada* are you, *amorcita*? Are you going to pretend that the good Señor Tolland has the right to call you *amada*?

Come now, we both know better than that."
He touched her cheek and she flinched away,
as if his fingers were tipped with fire.

This was getting ridiculous, backing around
here in the darkened galley. Hardly a romantic spot, even if she and Lucian were not at
cross purposes.

"What are you thinking about, *amada*? I
can see those enormous eyes of yours glowing
in the darkness as if they were moonlight
seen through amber. Are you frightened of the
storm?"

Frightened of the storm! She had all but
forgotten about the threat outside, when here
in the hot, humid space was a threat of
another kind, a threat against which she had
no defenses at all!

"If you must know," she flung at him desperately, "I was thinking how silly we're
acting—you wishing you were marooned here
with Jill and me longing for Bill."

"Foolish *niña*, that is not at all what you
wish. Do you think I don't know when a
woman is interested in me as a man? Come
now, enough of these childish games. Why not
admit that you were simply leading poor
Tolland on in an effort to disguise your growing interest in me? You admit that it was not
to make your sister uncomfortable."

"What?" Hannah choked, hearing only that
he had guessed her secret. "Why you . . . I
wouldn't . . . !"

"Don't perjure yourself, *amada*. You are a
foolish *muchacha* who speaks before thinking

and now the time has come for us to stop pretending. Surely you did not imagine I would allow you to leave with your photographer friend? Do I seem to you the sort of man to waste his opportunities?"

"Ha! You're wasting one right now, whether you know it or not! Bill's so crazy about my stepsister that if it's humanly possible he'll talk her into going back to him, and you've given him a golden opportunity. You ran off and left them alone together at Cancun and you just might find yourself without a fiancée when we get back there tonight. Don't discount Bill Tolland, Lucian, just because he lacks some of your . . . your . . . well, anyway, he has more kindness and understanding in his little finger than you.".

"You do it every time, don't you, *amada*?" Even in the darkness she could see him shaking his head and she was stung by his tone of voice. He wasn't even taking her seriously!

"Just you wait and see, Lucian Trent! This time you've outsmarted yourself, so don't come crying to me when we get back and find Jill all starry-eyed about Bill! He won her once before, so he can do it again!"

"And they will have my sincere congratulations," he promised smoothly.

"That's why he flew all this way and Jill knows it, too, because . . . What did you say?" Her voice dropped down to a whisper as his words sunk in.

"How far back in our conversation shall I

go?" he asked, amusement clear in his voice. "I have an idea you have not heard anything I have said in the past five minutes, you were so intent on throwing up a protective barrier of words. Do you believe such a flimsy barrier will protect you now, *pobrecita*? You should know me better."

His hands closed over her shoulders and Hannah felt her knees almost give way as he hauled her close to him. One hand slid down her back to press her hips tightly against his hard thighs and the tension in the air was electric, a measurable thing that charged every cell in her body. "I don't know what you mean, Lucian," she whispered just before his mouth cut off her pitiful words.

"Open your mouth," he commanded her, taking her bottom lip between his thumb and forefinger to break through her last stubborn defense. As he tasted the sweetness, exploring sensuously, suggestively, he shook her in an effort to break through the stiffened resistance. She was burningly conscious of the hard, flat muscles and the elastic skin that rose above his low-riding jeans and even as every fiber of her being was drawn to his magnetism, she held out, her arms hanging limply at her sides. She was in no position to use those arms to fight back when one of his hands slipped under her shirt to move slowly over her sensitized skin, finding and cupping her breast with stunning tenderness. She could feel her taut nipple as it probed the palm of his hand and the contact telegraphed frantic messages throughout her body. When she whimpered a protest under the gentle persuasion of his mouth, instead of desisting, he picked her up and carried her easily the few feet into the larger of the two staterooms, to lower her onto the bed.

"Lucian, please," she whispered desperately.

"All right, *enamorada,* be patient."

She heard the soft rustle of cloth and the muted thud as his jeans struck the vinyl deck and then he was beside her, lying on top of the coarsely woven spread.

"Yo te amo, mi pajarita," he whispered, claiming her lips once more.

Helplessly, her hands fluttered up to his shoulders, her fingers losing themselves in the thickness of his hair and then, as she felt him tugging at her sleeve, pulling the shirt from her arms, she began to protest.

Immediately, he stopped her with a kiss, his mouth moving slowly against her own, lifting, nibbling, playing with her as he ignited brush-fires that threatened to burn out of control. When he finally released her lips, he slipped the shirt over her head before she could protest and then, when she felt his mouth move down to claim her throbbing breasts, his tongue flicking tantalizing circles around the engorged tips, she was beyond reason, beyond knowing anything except for this wild, singing power that drove her to the edges of consciousness. She was driven relentlessly to press herself against his hard, hair-roughened body. "Oh, Lucian . . . I love you so terribly," she sighed, taking his hand to kiss each fingertip before placing it back on her breast.

"Do you, *amada*?" He smiled through the darkness. He was a shadow above her as he settled his body heavily over her own. "You still have on too many clothes." Even as he spoke, his hands were busy at her drawstring and he slipped her pants down easily over her hips. "I'll try not to hurt you, *querida mía*," he groaned against her throat, "but oh, I want you so much . . . so very much more than I have ever wanted anything before." His hands were arousing her to a fever pitch and her head thrashed mindlessly on the pillow, lost to everything except for this overpowering need he aroused in her, a need that could only be fulfilled by Lucian himself.

"You're not frightened of me, are you, my darling one?"

"Oh, Lucian, yes . . . no . . . oh, I don't know! Please, just love me now."

She felt his hand on her inner thigh, his thumb—and then he seemed to freeze. Somewhere in the most obscure corner of her mind Hannah was dimly aware of a sound coming from outside the warm darkness around them, as if a thousand bees were swarming, and Lucian swore under his breath and raised himself to stand beside the bunk. She could see the breadth of his shoulders against the cold light that now poured in through the porthole and then he leaned down and picked up his jeans, snapping them on even as he left the room.

Hannah felt as if every nerve in her body were screaming. Dazed, she lay there in the stillness, feeling the air move caressingly over her nakedness where only seconds before Lucian had breathed the fire of life itself. She was only dimly conscious of the voices from outside and it was not until she heard the noise again, a noise she now recognized as an outboard motor, heard Lucian call out a *gracias* to someone called Benenzio, that she moved.

Then she dragged herself up and felt around for her clothes and, taking them with her, she closed herself in the small bathroom. She didn't bother turning on a light as she dressed herself. Her hair was a hopeless tangle and her comb was—Lord knows where! She splashed cold water over her face and wrists and, taking a deep breath, she let herself out.

Lucian was just coming through the door. He carried a flashlight which, fortunately, he kept trained on the floor, for she couldn't have borne to have him see her now. How could she possibly have forgotten herself to such an extent? What must he think of her utterly abandoned behavior? He couldn't help but know that she was a more-than-willing participant, and if it hadn't been for the interruption, she would have been completely his by now. Not that she had tried to disguise her feelings—she had even revealed her love for him in words!

Thank heaven for Benenzio, whoever he was! Even as her mind was telling what a narrow escape she had had, her body was crying out desperately for what it had so nearly known and now never would.

"I think perhaps we should have a drink, *amada*," Lucian told her quietly, holding the light so as to guide her steps down the companionway.

"I think we'd better skip the drink and get back to Cancun to pick up the others," she retorted. Was that hoarse voice hers? It sounded as if it hadn't been used in a year!

"Have you heard nothing I've been telling you, *amada*?"

"Don't call me that!" she flared at him, fighting against tears of anger, frustration, and disappointment. Oh, yes, definitely disappointment. For the rest of her empty life she would regret not having known Lucian's love. Even one night to carry hidden in her heart through the coming years would be preferable to the pain of nothingness.

"Come, we will go on deck now. The storm has passed and there is a coolness in the air we could both use at the moment." He led her out into the night, and by the light of a waxing moon she could see the silhouette of a small boat as it snaked its way past the twin cliffs that guarded their sanctuary.

Wordlessly, he poured her a drink and handed it to her and she drank deeply, nearly strangling. "What is it?" she sputtered.

"Brandy."

"I was expecting wine," she breathed, blinking away the sudden tears brought on by the strength of the spirits.

"There is a time for wine and a time for brandy. The stronger drink for compensation, perhaps, no?"

There was no mistaking his meaning and she withdrew herself into a small bundle, tucking her feet up beneath her on the bench that ran alongside the cockpit.

"Benenzio saw us running before the storm and wanted to assure himself that we were safe. His timing was deplorable, but that, of course, I did not tell him."

"No, you thanked him. I heard you. Well, he has my thanks, too, for what it's worth. The wine . . . the storm . . ." She stumbled to an embarrassed halt, unable to think of anything else to blame her behavior on.

"No, *amor mía*, not the wine and not the storm. In spite of your silly pretenses, I have known you were attracted to me." He raised a staying hand. "No, no, before you fly at me once more like the little *tizón*, the firebrand, that you are, let me assure you that this is not conceit on my part. Any mature male knows when a woman looks on him with favor, *carina*, and in this case I was doubly aware because the attraction was mutual."

Hannah caught her breath and put the glass down dangerously near the edge. "You mean you . . ."

"Yes, I mean I was drawn to you from the very first, *mi pajarita*, for I had just come

from the *casa* where I had been informed by
Jill that a young relative of hers had taken the
opportunity to drop in unexpectedly, hoping
for a place to visit during her vacation. I
found, instead of the brash young opportunist
I expected, a very young, very beautiful and
also very frightened-looking girl who had
seemingly broken into my private workroom
and wrecked something that I had worked on
for hours."

"Oh, but . . ."

"I know, I know, *amada*, that out of the
tenderness of your heart, you allowed me to
believe what was not true. Then, as your
sister saw my growing interest in our visitor,
she filled my ears with still more information.
For instance, did I not know that this was the
very woman who had broken up her marriage?" He shrugged his shoulders expres-
sively. "Your sister pleads a very convincing
case, Hannah, and I was on guard on her
behalf, especially after she told me that even
now you were sharing a house with this man."

"Oh, no! How could she?"

"Women, *amor mía*, are quick to revert to a
primitive state when their love is threatened,
and at that time I believe your sister thought
her best interests lay in my direction."

Bristling, Hannah jumped to the defense of
her sex. "Oh, and I suppose men don't?"

"Hmm, well, I'll have to admit to the odd
impulse to commit murder when you began to
shower attention on Tolland. I began to believe Jill's tales were based on fact after all."

"After all? You mean you doubted her word?" Hope put a lilt back in Hannah's voice and she picked up her half-empty glass and sipped cautiously at the fiery liquid. Something in her needed a bit of strengthening, whether it was her trembling body or her moral fiber.

"One of the blessings that comes with age and experience, *amorcita,* is the ability to judge character. I began to be intrigued by the discrepancies between the open, carefree young woman who so quickly enchanted my children and the calculating creature who waited until her sister's back was turned to move in on her helpless husband. I watched you with interest, *amada,* and I scarcely even noticed when interest turned to liking and liking to loving—perhaps because all along, my emotions had been disguised by plain old straightforward desire," he added dryly.

He stood up as he spoke those last words and now he was before her, moving in to block her escape, as if she even wanted to escape what she sensed would be his next move. Perhaps it was the brandy on top of the wine; whatever it was, Hannah was determined not to waste a second chance.

"Just one thing, though . . . what about Jill?" she asked him now, staying him with a none-too-steady hand on his bare chest. "I mean, aren't you engaged or something like that—at least unofficially? How will she feel when we tell her . . .?" Her voice trailed off uncertainly. Tell her what? That Lucian wanted to have an affair on the side, a last fling before settling down to the bonds of matrimony?

"Stop it, Hannah. I can see the thoughts racing around in that foolish little mind of yours and they are not worthy of you. Do you really think I want to have an affair with the sister of my *novia*? With the woman who cares for my own children? Surely you know me better than that."

"I—I don't really know anything, Lucian, except that . . ."

"Except that?" he prompted. "Say it, *amada*." He touched her hair and then let his fingers trail around to cup her chin, lifting her face up to his. "Say it," he whispered.

There came the cry of a *chachalaka*, a fierce, almost human cry that shattered the silence, and the bird winged over the small harbor. Neither of the occupants of the boat stirred, nor did their eyes waver as Lucian willed her to speak.

"I—I love you," she whispered intensely, then, in a rush. "But you know that. I told you before, when we . . . when . . . and anyway, you said you knew how I felt all along. You were probably laughing at me, sharing the joke with Jill when I—when Bill and I . . ."

"When you pretended to be so cool toward me? When later on you pretended to be, oh, so fascinated by the good Señor Tolland?" There was a touch of laughter in his voice even now but it was kind laughter. "Ah, no, *amorcita*, I never laughed at you. Lusted after you, perhaps—that I cannot deny—but laughed at you? Never." He took her by the hand and led her, unresisting, to the other side of the cockpit, where a cushion, wet with dew and rain, lay tossed on the bench. Disregarding the wetness, he pulled her down onto his lap and pressed her head back against his throat. "I see I must clear up this matter of my persistent visitor or you will never let it rest. I met Jill in London, and as I was at loose ends, we saw something of each other for a while— all very superficial, you understand, very social." His tone of voice left her in no doubt as to his opinion of the London social scene that had thrilled Jill so much. "When it became necessary for me to return to the island to care for my children, she very graciously offered to come along and lend a hand. Your sister is a very lovely woman, *amada*, and I could find no objection, even knowing as I did that she was interested in a more permanent arrangement. I have not reached the age of thirty-four without learning how to protect myself from determined women."

Hannah cast him a sidelong glance of inquiry but his only response was to tighten the arms around her in a manner that was infinitely satisfying.

"You mean you really didn't want to marry her? Not at all?" she asked, having trouble with the rapid readjustment of her ideas.

"Not at all after the first few days. I admit I

examined the idea, for you know my children need a mother, but unless she is the woman I adore, it would not be a successful union. Your sister and I were never in love, although she was attracted to what she considered my style of living."

"And it really isn't your style of living? Do you mean the London thing or here—on Co-zumel—I mean, with the ruins and the horses and the children?" It was important to her, for into one life she could never in a million years fit with ease and into the other she had already nestled down with a contentment that could last forever.

"You don't have to ask, *amada*. You have ridden with me in the freshness of a new day, you have remained silent with me where ages ago my ancestors watched and worshipped. My children adore you, as you do them. Could ever a man ask for more? You have seen the *casa* I am having built on the other side of the island—seen it with Tolland, unfortunately." He shook her playfully and nipped at her nape, wounding only to soothe with his tongue. "Why did you have to invite him here, although I must admit he has finally served a useful purpose."

"But I didn't, Lucian. He just came any-way," she hastened to assure him.

"Hmm, that is even better." His lips were exploring her ears now and she could scarcely pay attention to what he was saying. "I thought perhaps you had imported him as a counterirritant to make me pay you more attention." His words were teasing and she answered in the same vein.

"Conceited! You think the whole world revolves around you!"

"Ah, no, *enamorada*, the world has revolved around a small, fiery package of womanhood for almost a month now. If I have any conceit at all it is that you would consent to spend the rest of your life with me."

"There, you see? You're even taking my consent for granted now, aren't you?" She gasped delightfully and shifted to avoid his exploring hands.

"Hmmm, but I have ways to assure your consent. You, who would not think of living in the house with Bill Tolland without the presence of his mother—how would you like to spend several days alone with me aboard the *Sunbird*? Would you consider yourself compromised enough to marry me?" He pushed her down on the bench and she caught her breath as the cold, wet plastic touched her bare skin. This shirt of Lucian's was altogether too easy to remove!

"Would you care to try me and see?" she challenged, tracing the line of his lips with an unsteady finger.

"Fortunately, we have no choice. The generators are not working and thus we have no lights. Did you know, *amor mía*, that it is illegal to run at night without lights?" His hands were driving the meaning of his words from her mind. "So you see, my sweet captive, you will have to marry me as soon as we return to the island."

"I wish we were married now," she whispered shyly.

Her words seemed to inflame him and he turned her so that she was lying on top of him. "It will be just as soon as I make the arrangements, *querida mía*. I suppose somewhere we'll have to find the time to rescue the Tollands from Cancun."

"And the children . . ."

". . . may as well remain where they are, for they will be with the Maitlands while we honeymoon."

"Honeymoon . . . oh, Lucian, could we . . . ?"

Her words were closed off and by the time she could speak again she had forgotten what it was she had wanted to say.

Silhouette Romance

ROMANCE THE WAY
IT USED TO BE...
AND COULD BE AGAIN

Contemporary romances for today's women.

Each month, six very special love stories will be yours

from SILHOUETTE.

Look for them wherever books are sold

or order now from the coupon below.

$1.50 each